Second Wives

Second Wives

The Silent Struggle

Christine Thomas

Fender Publishing Company

Seattle Washington

ISBN: 0-9640354-5-6   SAN 298-1750

Library of Congress Cataloging-in-Publication Data

Thomas, Christine, 1953-
        Second wives : the silent struggle / Christine Thomas.
        p.   cm.
        Includes bibliographical references (p. 154).
        ISBN 0-9640354-5-6
        1. Wives--Psychology.   2. Remarried people--Psychology.
    I. Title.
HQ759.T448   1999   98-38577
306.84--dc21   CIP

Books from Fender Publishing Company are distributed by BookWorld Services, Inc. To order additional copies, please call 800-444-2524.

Printed in the United States of America

This book is dedicated to my family who told me that I could do it, especially my husband who still doesn't have his kitchen back.

Contents

Note to the Reader

The advice, recommendations, jokes, and other assorted proclamations in this book represent the personal opinions of the writer and, by extension, the publisher. However, neither the writer nor the publisher is responsible for any re-actions, events, legal or personal experiences that might be inspired by this book. The purpose of this book is to entertain and provide information. This book is not subject to any outside governmental or legal review process. Neither is it a manipulative tool of the totalitarian Establishment, the hungry hounds of political correctness, or America's drab and sappy corporate media machine.

If you have opinions that differ from the ones in this book or you would simply like to correspond with a cool publisher like us, we would like to hear from you. Write to Fender Publishing Company, 1111 East Madison, Suite 460, Seattle, WA 98122.

Does the road wind up-hill all the way?
Yes, to the very end.
Will the day's journey take the whole long day?
From morn to night, my friend.

Christina Rossetti

Second Wives

~*Introduction*~

S econd wives happen to be a fact of life, especially in our day and age. First wives divorce their husbands. First wives have affairs, and their husbands divorce them. With the divorce rate in this country at approximately 50 percent, chances are that every other married woman you meet is a second wife.

This is the millennium after all, so why is there still such a social stigma attached to being the second wife? Does being first in line somehow make a person superior? Second wives, as a whole, have been cast aside by society, stereotyped, scorned, and held in derision. First wives get all the glory and sympathy, as we well know from the movies, the media, and the attitudes of the mindless masses.

Today's second wife faces not only society's scorn, but a variety of possible situations that would challenge even the most resourceful and energetic woman on earth. She might, for example, find herself in any one of numerous situations. She could be a never-married woman who marries a divorced man with children from a former marriage. She could be a divorced woman without children, who marries a man with children from a former marriage. In either of these instances, her husband probably will not have custody of his children . . . but he might.

Alternatively, a second wife might be a divorced woman with children of her own children from her first marriage who marries a man with children of his own, who does not have custody. She could even be a divorced grandmother who marries a younger man with children still living at home.

For many wives, a first marriage is their husband's second. If so, he might be carrying around some extra baggage due to the effects of his divorce. If both husband and wife have been married and divorced, each might have an extra bag or two.

Let's say she has children from a former marriage, but he does not. Is he prepared to walk into the role of instant father? What if he has children, but she does not? She'll be married-with-children before you can say the word "sitcom." If both have children, how does each feel about the other's children? Will their kids even like each other? What if they don't? This is just the tip of the "iceberg of family issues" that most second wives face.

As we grapple with these different scenarios, we attempt simultaneously to deal with society's stereotypes. Yes, we're all very familiar with the stereotypes and assumptions. A young second wife is a bimbo. An older second wife is either a gold digger or a cradle robber. If the second wife met her husband before his divorce was final, she's a home-wrecker. And, god forbid, she's good-looking! Then she's a trophy wife. Looks *can* kill, I guess.

These assumptions are part of the propaganda created by first wives and all the folks out there who fear divorce. Why should a beautiful, young second wife be anyone's worst nightmare? She didn't cause the breakdown of the first marriage. She is simply one outcome of it.

Attitudes about the images of the brazen home-wrecker and the evil stepmother never fail to make their way into the daily lives of second wives. We know they're not true. I've never met a second wife who felt like a trophy. Although compared to first wives in terms of character, many of the husbands would probably consider their second wives great rewards for having survived against all odds. Perhaps they deserve trophies!

Stereotypes and the remarks that people make do hurt. We know they're not true, but we feel the effects of the insults anyway. Anyone who is cast down by society feels it, and second wives are no exception. However, as you read on, you will find that many second wives have their own special defense weapons to use in the battle against the close-minded attitudes of nosy neighbors and others with nasty attitudes.

While we're defending ourselves against the outside world, we're also struggling to make our marriages work. Everyone has at least one or two problems in her marriage, let's face it. Second marriages have all the same challenges and issues as first marriages, plus quite a few more. Some people remarry before they are completely over their divorces, bringing a host of unresolved problems into the new relationship. Many a second wife, suddenly thrust into the dramatic role of stepmother, stumbles at first as she tries to find the right balance for herself, for the kids, and for their father.

Fairy tales such as *Cinderella, Snow White,* and *Hansel and Gretel* have done nothing for the image of stepmothers. These stories have perpetuated the idea of the stepmother as an evil, wicked woman who has little regard for the welfare of her stepchildren. Although centuries old, this image of the wicked stepmother has been deeply drilled into our subconscious.

Anna

"Many of the negative connotations we have as adults started way back when we were all too young to know the truth (that not all stepmothers are evil) and too powerless to do anything about it."

Another possible contribution to the negative image of stepmothers, although not commonly known, is the original definition of the word "step." The root of the word "step" dates back to the Old English word "stoep," which means "deprived." Back then, stepchildren were thought of as deprived because a woman other than their own biological mother was raising them.

These factors, conscious and unconscious, current and historical, combine to create a difficult situation for today's second wife. The stress can seem overwhelming. Financial difficulties are often monumental due to biased laws and judges who put the whole burden of child support solely upon the divorced father. Many second wives cope daily with ex-wives-from-hell, whom we will be discussing at length in a later chapter.

"People were very offended when I married John," Yoko Ono said of her marriage to John Lennon. Fans had formed a fond image of John and his first wife which was tarnished by their divorce. The public seemed offended then, not only that John and Yoko were in love, but that they dared to flaunt their love publicly. Eventually, they were driven into a reclusive life, having little contact with the media for many years.

Later Yoko Ono emerged much stronger; she stands as a inspiration to second wives everywhere. And so we must each ask ourselves, how will we emerge? Will our blended families actually blend? Will our marriages endure? How will we fit into this family-centered society with our newly configured reconstructed families?

Blended families are often much bigger, and more complicated. Let us not forget the tangential members, such as the step-grandparents, step-aunts, step-uncles, and step-cousins. Only recently has some research begun into the dynamics of blended families and how they differ from biofamilies. The ongoing and interconnected relationships in stepfamilies are difficult for many people to understand, even those with experience in family counseling. Very few psychologists, psychiatrists, and counselors are up-to-date on the unique educational and therapeutic programs that could be helpful for stepfamilies.

Second wives face colossal challenges, finding themselves in the uncharted territories of today's changing society. Most of the second wives interviewed for this book feel alienated, somehow, from the mainstream. Some feel as if they are not only second wives, they are second-class citizens as well. Often, they don't know where to look for help or advice. In our conversations, many of the women seemed to feel very alone, indeed, overwhelmed by their situations. Some of the second wives even felt that their husbands didn't understand their feelings.

Julia

"I've often felt that stepparents, and particularly stepmothers, have an enormous burden that is largely unrecognized by anyone who is not going through it. I am fed up with all these sob stories about the horrible lives of saintly single mothers and the tragedy caused by deadbeat dads. What about those second wives who can never have any children of their own because of their husbands' child support payments? The courts have deemed those children more important than any children the second wives might have. What about all those divorced fathers who faithfully pay child support every time it is due only to see their ex-wives use it for frivolous items like liposuction or vacations to Europe? What about those blended families who will struggle with higher education expenses because Dad didn't have the ability to save due to child support payments? What about all the blended families who struggle trying to put the kids through school because all the child support has been spent long before the child turned 18, by an ex-wife who doesn't give a damn if the kids go to college or not?"

The common perception about divorced fathers is that they don't do much for their children.

Jane

"How can they when the court has reduced their role to nothing more than a source of money? I wish there was some way to ensure that the money paid by fathers actually went to the children. I think courts tire easily of child custody issues and don't always recognize how valuable it is for children to have contact with both parents as much as possible. There is truly a void of information and help for women in my circumstances."

Why such estrangement? Why such disparate treatment? Why such unfair treatment? These questions and others will be addressed now in this book. Together we will examine the issues that second wives face on a daily basis. We'll try to put these issues into perspective, as well as to steer second wives and stepmothers towards information and assistance.

This is a book of thoughts and ideas for second wives everywhere. Many second wives from coast to coast have offered statements expressing their personal feelings and giving advice to other second wives. Their goal, like mine, is to help all of us explore the silent struggle that millions of women endure as second wives; moreover, to bring this experience out into the open so that women like us can talk about this book and our lives, sharing feelings, experiences, and dreams with one another.

1
~Welcome to the Nightmare~

You've met him, the man of your dreams. He's everything you have ever hoped for in a husband. He's kind, loving, funny, generous, helpful. After kissing all those toads, finally you've fallen in love. As the relationship develops, you learn more and more about each other's past. You find out he's divorced. Oh, wonderful. Well, at least you know he can commit. But then he begins to tell you a little about his ex-wife and, day by day, the story just gets worse and worse.

Then one day, he gets angry at you out of the blue and you suspect that his anger is coming from the past.

"Where's my screwdriver, Mary?"

"Oh, I used it to fix the hinge on the cupboard door this morning. I thought I put it back in your toolbox."

"Well, you didn't. How many times do I have to tell you to leave my toolbox alone? If you need something fixed, tell me and I'll fix it. You know I can't stand my tools being disorganized. My ex-wife was always misplacing and disorganizing my tools."

"Sorry."

"You're always sorry."

"Damn it. Quit yelling at me. I did tell you. And besides, I've been telling you every day for the last month. Maybe if you'd listen to me sometime instead of sitting on your ass in front of the television every damn night when you get home from work, I wouldn't have to touch your precious tool box."

We've all had petty fights like this. They start with a stupid little issue and, the next thing you know, the two of you aren't even speaking to each other. Past relationships affect present relationships, sometimes in unpredictable ways. This is true whether we want to admit it or not. We all carry some extra baggage around, if it's just a small overnight bag or a giant suitcase. Something went wrong with his first relationship or you wouldn't be with him now. So, what went wrong? Was it him? Was it her? Was it just a bad combination?

Whatever happened, the man has scars. He's got issues. He's carrying around that extra baggage and once in a while he's bound to dump it on you. Bear in mind, however, that he didn't let the horror of his last marriage stop him from taking another chance. Remember, he is not with *her,* he's with *you.*

Your job is to be understanding and not let what happened to him in the past affect your new relationship. This is a tough job. It's a job that nobody would want if she weren't in love. Whatever the circumstances surrounding his divorce, the important thing is that you are not her. You are you. This is an important point you must get across to him, before you get to the point of hitting him over the head with a frying pan. Hopefully, he'll listen.

Maybe both of you have been married and divorced. You both have extra baggage to lug around. Your ex-husband left you with your own hang-ups and hassles. Remember the first petty fight and how it started? It's easy to lose it over stupid shit sometimes.

For example, suppose that your ex was a total slob. As a result, you can't stand someone who doesn't pick up after himself. After all, you don't ask for much, just a little cooperation now and then. He's not helpless, nor is he an invalid. When you walk in the door at night, tired from working all day, the last thing you want to see is a stack of dirty dishes in the sink, wet towels on the floor in the bathroom, or dirty clothes next to the hamper.

"Can't you just once put the dishes in the dishwasher? Is that too much to ask?"

"Well, hello, dear. How was your day?"

"Don't be a smart ass. Damn it, you know how much it irritates me to come home to a messy house. You get home from work before I do. I'm tired of being treated like I'm nothing more than a live-in maid around here. My ex was so lazy he couldn't even put his dirty dishes in the sink, much less the dishwasher."

Before the two of you get to this point over minor irritations, you should sit down together, talk to each other, and discuss a few minor details. For example, what did each of you expect from marriage? Have you ever thought about it? Most people tend to have certain expectations, spoken or unspoken, conscious or unconscious, of their relationships. These expectations, acknowledged or not, can lead to eventual disappointment and then to most of the problems in a marriage. Most people expect love and companionship. For others, plenty of good sex is high up on the list. Some of us expect to have children. What is it that you personally expect from marriage? Have you and your husband ever sat down and discussed your expectations?

Let's talk about love. You are in love with your husband or you wouldn't be in this mess now. There is no other rational explanation. But has love ever been rational? Have you ever thought about the definition of the word love? What exactly is love? In the game of tennis, love is a score of zero. Maybe more of us should play tennis. We wouldn't be so surprised at all the zeroes in our lives!

Love is a fundamental and necessary human need. We all want to love that someone special, as well as to be loved and accepted in return by that same someone special. George Sand once said, "There is only one happiness in life—to love and be loved." Most of us hope to achieve this special love through our relationship with our husbands. Many people, however, are not prepared to deal with the problems encountered in romantic relationships. The high divorce rate in this country is proof enough of our inadequacy in this area.

What to do? You've all heard the old saying, "Knowledge is power." How can you gain the necessary knowledge to have a successful marriage? One way is to carefully examine the relationships of other couples you know, including that of your parents. Are they happy? If so, how do they behave towards each other? Are they miserable, constantly complaining about each other? If they're unhappy, exactly what is it that irritates the wife about her husband? What does the wife do to annoy her husband?

Sara

"As you get older you realize that those things you hear when you're a teenager are such a joke! Love does not conquer all and you cannot live on love. But love has to be there or what is it all for?"

Love makes us happy, puts a spring in our step, a smile on our face, and gives us a reason to live. Life without love is barren and empty. Most people crave love. Marriage, then, is the ultimate fulfillment of the desire for love.

Love also hurts. Love requires a lot of work and energy for it to remain strong. Love is not something to take for granted, for it is easily destroyed. That's probably the reason that the divorce rate is so damn high. People fall in love, get married, and think that they are going to live happily ever after on their love without caring for the love itself.

For centuries, love itself was not even considered a requirement for marriage. In the olden days, marriages were arranged by parents. Usually, the bride and groom were not consulted as to whether or not they were in love. They were expected to marry each other, bear children, and fulfill their obligations to their parents and to their village. Marriage was basically a business contract. With any luck at all, love might enter into the picture. If they never did fall in love with each other, one or both just had an affair or suffered through it. Simple!

Thankfully, things have changed over the centuries. Love is the crux of marriage for most people. Marriage, however, requires more than just love to succeed and flourish. In real life there are all those minor technicalities to think about, such as: Who takes out the garbage? Who goes grocery shopping? Who puts the groceries away? Who earns the living? Who pays the bills? Who does the cooking? Who does the dishes? Who does the laundry? Who cleans the house? Who balances the checkbook? Can *anybody* balance the checkbook?

Then there are basic personality differences between husband and wife to consider. Two individuals with their own personal views of life, their unique likes and dislikes, living together and sleeping together every day are bound to have a disagreement every so often. How you handle those inevitable disagreements can contribute to the success or destruction of your marriage.

Some of the knowledge you've gained from prior relationships, whether those relationships were good or bad, can be put to use in building an excellent relationship with the new love of your life. Have you ever analyzed the reasons behind your divorce? Were you in love when you married or did you just drink too much and wake up in Vegas with a new last name? What was it that went wrong? What about your husband's previous marriage? What problems led to his divorce? Have you and your husband ever talked about your prior relationships at all? It's not easy for many people to talk about these things, especially if there are bitter memories.

Esther

"He was very honest about the situation starting with the first date. We both knew right away that our relationship would probably last so we were very careful to communicate fully about his child and her mother."

Love, however, is more than just talking to each other. It's a meeting of the souls, an attempt to make a life, and a joining together of two dreams.

Amy

"Certainly if we are divorced, we couldn't live with our ex's, and we couldn't see eye to eye. What we need to do is get beyond that point, let go, and do the best we can for ourselves and our children."

Many times, our expectations for marriage are based upon our childhood experiences. For some of us, this can be a very positive backdrop for our adult life but, for others, it can be downright hurtful or even dangerous.

For example, a woman who grew up without a father or a male role model in her life might subconsciously be looking for a father figure instead of a husband. Then, rather than contributing to her marriage, she might expect to have everything provided for her, as if she were a child.

A man who grew up with an abusive father or stepfather probably did not have a good example from which to learn about the joys of being a husband or a father. A woman who grew up with a cold or angry father might think that it's okay for a man to abuse his wife and children, not ever having seen or experienced anything different.

If these adults were never able to overcome or understand their childhood difficulties, they might end up picking the wrong husband or wife. So many families with so many problems! No wonder we have a whole new vocabulary to deal with them. "Dysfunctional" is the one word that comes to mind. Therefore, it should be no surprise that such a high percentage of marriages result in unhappy relationships and eventually in divorce.

We are often too quick to look for excuses or to blame other groups besides our own for social ills, such as divorce or illegitimate children. Society is not so quick to look for solutions to these problems, however. Each and every one of us, as a member of the society in which we live, carries some of the blame and responsibility for these problems.

As adults, we should be mature enough to put aside childish emotions and learn to communicate better with each other. If we don't, any relationship we might find ourselves in will be doomed from the very beginning. If we refuse to take the necessary time to understand and make known our thoughts and feelings, then we all must share the blame for society's problems, including divorce. It's easy to just blame divorce on men, but it's not that simple. We are all adults and we are all responsible.

Most people fail to think about reality when considering marriage. Remember, they're in love and, after all, isn't love supposed to conquer all? Marriage is a choice we make as to the person with whom we will live, love, and raise a family. Why do we find it so hard to discuss our expectations from the relationship? Could it be that we, as women, are afraid that we won't get that ring on our finger if we talk about these things in advance? Are we trying to convince our husbands-to-be that life will be a bed of roses? If so, the fault lies right at our feet, especially if the reality of the marriage ends up being totally different from what we promised it would be.

Marriage is a combination of love and business. Most people would hesitate at doing business with their friends, but don't think twice about doing business with their lovers. The trick is how to combine love and business and survive, maybe even thrive when all is said and done.

You and your husband love each other above all. You will face many obstacles together. You already know this, in your heart. The only thing that is going to see the two of you through all of it is your love. Tell him every day, at least once a day, that you love him! Cherish your love, guard it, and treasure it. You will be rewarded.

Jeanie

"It was love at first sight and I'm grateful to his ex for not having the insight to treasure the wonderful man she had the privilege of being married to for over 15 years."

Becky

"At first I was a little leery about getting involved with a guy who had so much baggage, so to speak. But he persisted and I eventually fell in love with him and with the kids."

Second marriages are far more complicated when children are involved. Mae West once said, "Marriage is a great institution, but I'm not ready for an institution." If you're a second wife, maybe an institution is just the place for you!

If you're not a second wife yet, maybe you and he are living together. Let's take a couple of minutes to talk about cohabitation. Cohabitation is the politically correct way of saying "living together" or, as in the olden days, "shacking up." "Shacking up" makes it sound like you're doing something wrong, which usually turns out to be a whole lot of fun. Maybe that's the reason behind the current trend to be politically correct—someone out there doesn't want us to have any fun!

The one benefit of living together is that if it doesn't work out at least you don't have to go through the financial expense of getting a divorce. You can just pack up and leave or put all his clothes in a garbage bag and throw them out the window at him when he comes home from work. Seems easy and uncomplicated? Notice that I said "financial expense," because there will definitely be an emotional cost, especially if you've been together for any length of time. There will also be even more emotional cost if there are children involved and you've grown attached to them and they to you. However, breaking up will not be as traumatic as divorce and that's why some women hesitate to tie the knot with a previously married man.

Many, possibly most, second wives have married their husbands totally unaware of the difficulties that divorced fathers face, and even more unprepared for the problems they would face as stepmothers. They overlooked the impact that an interfering and jealous ex-wife could have on their marriage. Nobody mentioned that paying child support to a former wife could be an obstacle to their financial well-being. These second wives weren't prepared to deal with custody and visitation issues. They fell in love and got married, and didn't think about the reality of the situation.

Perhaps living together first for a year or two is a good idea. At least the second wife would get a first-hand look at the life of a second wife without making that wholehearted commitment right off the bat. You don't want to be caught unawares and end up regretting the whole damn thing. Some second wives are very up-front about their decisions to get married before they knew what was ahead. Would they have been better off just living together?

Linda

"I had my doubts entering the marriage, but went ahead with it anyway, believing our love could conquer all! I can't take it anymore. I should *never* have married him."

Pearl

"I have been married (this is my second time) for three years. I swore when I got divorced the first time I would never marry again. I wish I had stuck to it."

Genevieve

"My husband never forgave his first wife for leaving him for another man. No matter what I did, he never felt secure. He just could not seem to manage his jealous feelings. Since his first wife had left him, he really thought that I would leave him as well.

"His ex-wife always managed to prevent him from having a normal relationship with his children. We finally managed to obtain regular visitation with his children, but only after many court battles and over $10,000 spent for lawyer's fees and court costs. Since my husband had been deprived of seeing his children for so many years, he let the kids walk all over him, getting mad at me when I would try to discuss discipline with him. His jealousy and anxiety tore him and our marriage apart."

Beth

"I went into the relationship wearing rose-colored glasses. I don't wear them anymore."

I'm not trying to scare you. After all, if you're living with the man you love and the only thing you're missing is the ring on your finger, then you're already dealing with all the same problems that come with being a second wife. You could look at it that way. If you're just dating, then perhaps you don't know what real life will be like. But if you're living together, you already have a pretty good idea. The decision is yours to make.

Everyone is well aware that the divorce rate for first marriages is 50 percent. However, in a *Money* (December 2, 1996) article, "The Brady Bunch of the 1990's," the statistical divorce rate for second marriages is estimated at 60 percent. Regardless of where the data for this estimate came from, it is a statistic that is often thrown around by the media. It doesn't really matter, though. Like so many statistics in the media, the motivation behind the number is usually political. Besides, even seemingly discouraging statistics don't always have be construed in a negative context. This 60 percent figure would simply mean that 40 percent or more of second marriages *are* successful.

Determination, hard work, and lots of love will see you through the rough spots. Wouldn't you like to grow old with the man you love? Is there anything else that could bring as much satisfaction as a warm, loving relationship with your husband and family? What material possession is there that could make you and your husband happier than to see your children and stepchildren grow up and live happy, successful lives of their own, pursuing their dreams?

Carol

"My fiancé and I have been living together for five years. We're talking about setting the date for our marriage. This will be the second marriage for both of us. We have fought about everything, dealt with insecurities, and we are still together. My advice to other women who might find themselves in this position is: do not to *rush* into marriage."

Marguerite

"Be honest and straightforward about *everything*. It's hard to do sometimes and there *will* be disagreements. How you choose to settle your disagreements is what's most important. It's okay to be angry with each other. Above all, remember that you love each other and keep that uppermost in your mind. The rest will fall into place."

The happiest second wives are the ones who took their time getting into a relationship with a divorced man and gave serious thought to the complications involved. Some are even delighted, grateful, and happy to be with the men they love, regardless of the difficulties and troubles that the relationship brings. For some women, love is the most important thing.

Cheryl

"Remember, if his ex has custody, she has most of the control regarding visitation with his kids. If she's a bitch and changes or denies visitation at the drop of a hat, your husband's anger and frustration are going to affect your relationship. We talked about *everything*—why he got divorced in the first place, how he feels when he doesn't get to see his son—and he agreed to let me help him through the rough spots and promised never to take his anger out on me. It's worked for the past twelve years and I don't regret one minute."

Whatever you believed in the past or whatever your feminist background, you must and will become aware of one basic truth: Laws are biased in favor of the biological mother, no matter what, plain and simple. If your husband-to-be has children, more than likely it's his ex-wife who has custody. The courts in our country award custody to the mother a full 95 percent of the time.

Practically the only way a biological mother will not get custody is if she is doing life in prison, no joke. These same biased laws allow divorced women with children to go on with their lives. A divorced woman with children, receiving child support, can remarry without fear. She doesn't have to worry about how she will feed her children. She is free to have more children in a future marriage. If she is receiving alimony (called "spousal support" to be politically correct and still liberally awarded these days), she is free to choose not to work. Of course, in almost all divorces, the ex-wife keeps the house and everything in it.

Depending on the ages of the children involved, a divorced father will have a sword hanging over his head for anywhere from 18 to 22 years. An ex-wife can take him back to court for an increase in child support anytime she gets in the mood, up until the child reaches the age of 18 (up to 22 if the child is in college or trade school). The harder he works, the more *she* gets. If your husband gets a raise, *she* runs back to the judge and gets that little bit extra that you and your family could really use.

For most of you, this is probably not news. In fact, most second wives learn the hard way that being a woman in a courtroom today is only an advantage for first wives. Perhaps you didn't realize this when you became a second wife, but it's something you soon learned. For those still contemplating marriage, you should really think it over. Not all of us are equipped to deal with the emotional strain of blatant injustice day in and day out.

You must be honest with your husband-to-be and honest with yourself. If you do get married, you'll see the injustice up close and personal and it may change every way you feel about marriage, women, and even being a citizen of this country. But remember, if you do choose to marry the love of your life, you will be a better woman for it and, compared to his ex, you will be *the* better woman.

Dana

"Absolutely no regrets whatsoever. The problems, and there have been many, have only brought us closer together."

Sandi

"I'm not going to say it hasn't been a long, hard road. It has. But I wouldn't trade my life with anyone else's. We lived together for a couple of years before we married. I think that helped bridge the gap and let us all get used to each other. We've experienced good times and bad. There were times I couldn't stand the thought of his kids coming to visit. I knew how important Tom's kids were to him, though, and that they were an important part of his life. He went out of his way to smooth the transition for the kids and myself. Our love for each other helped us get through it all."

2
~Living the Life~

*I*f you're reading this book, more than likely you are either a second wife, engaged to or dating a divorcé, or close to someone in the situation. Regardless, you have your personal reasons. I hope this book will help you reflect on your situation and perhaps think it through in new ways. At least you'll know that you are not alone!

As a second wife, you are an unusual individual. You've chosen to pursue a path in life that is different from those that other women might have chosen. Although some might think that your decision is peculiar, you made that choice for a special reason. Your husband is absolutely the greatest man you've ever met. If you're not a second wife but know someone who is, maybe you're reading this book to try to understand why someone would *choose* to be a second wife. Why not be first? Isn't it better to be first?

Laurel

"My husband once told me that he wished that we would have met each other first, before either of us had married our respective ex's. I told him that we wouldn't have been the people we are today. I'm able to really appreciate him. Everyday we are more in love."

Carla

"It's different the second time around. You realize that it really does take two to make the relationship work. You are both more mature and willing to compromise when necessary. You understand the importance of playing, working, and laughing together."

You might be rich. You might be poor. Maybe you're in-between. Regardless of your financial status, all second wives must face certain challenges. The utmost challenge seems to be dealing with the ex-wife-from-hell.

Monica

"Although our ex's may not have moved on with their emotional and psychological lives, my husband and I work hard every day to maintain serenity and sanity in our world. We take the time to wink, hold hands, kiss, and do something extra for each other every single day. Each of us is aware that our most important priority is each other."

You and your husband are in love and happily married. All of the complications involved in second marriages are nothing new to you. Your attitude is to let nothing and nobody interfere with your chosen life or your happiness. To hell with the stereotypes. You are determined to prove to the world that a second wife is not some sort of aberration. That's the right outlook to have.

There are a lot of unhappy people in the world who can't stand to see other people happy. Their sole purpose in life is to make everybody else as unhappy as they are. I figure if they spent half as much time and energy making their own lives and relationships happy as they do sticking their noses in your business and mine, they might not be so pathetically miserable.

If your husband's ex-wife is knocking herself out trying to make your life uncomfortable and interfering at every opportunity, there's no law that says that you have to let her succeed. Obviously, she has no life. If she had a life, she'd be busy living her life instead of spending her time trying to ruin yours. So, if you continue to be happy and content, working towards your goals and living your life the way you choose, despite all obstacles, this is better than any retaliation you could possibly dream up. You are spending your time productively, you are happy. This will piss off anybody, especially a bitter and unhappy ex-wife. Living well *is* the best revenge.

Carrie

"Early on, when the ex started fucking with us, we told ourselves that our best revenge was to be happy. We never stooped to her methods. Even though I was totally unprepared for the hatred that this woman would focus on me, I used her hatred to find a strength inside myself that I didn't know I had."

Cheryl

"My husband's ex harassed me constantly for the first year of our marriage. Because of my husband's love for me, I stayed strong. Not only do I have a wonderful, strong marriage, his kids now live with us and we all love every minute of it. Happiness is the best revenge."

Instead of letting her get to you, ignore her petty intrusions. Do everything that you can and do whatever you can, to not let her get to you. Keep telling yourself, "She has no life. I do." No matter how mad you get, never, ever, ever let her see you lose your cool, no matter how hard that might be.

Carrie

"Eventually, I was able to come to terms with most of the pettiness, and would tell other second wives that they should stick it out. Never give up."

Your financial affairs are nobody's business but your own. The ex-wife-from-hell, however, believes that any money available to her ex-husband should be available to her as well. For those of you whose husband's ex is nothing more than a blood-sucking leech, there are a few arrangements that other second wives have successfully used to keep their income and prior assets safely away from her money-grubbing hands. One is to keep separate bank accounts and to file taxes separately as well. It costs a little more, but the ex-wife cannot touch the money if your husband's name is not on the account.

Several second wives who owned their own homes before remarriage have set up trusts with the help of financial lawyers. The trust is the actual owner of the home. The trust can be set up so that you can be the trustee, and you are free to name another relative to be trustee in case of your death. Arrangements can be made so that your husband could continue to live in the house in the event of your death. If you want to sell or refinance, all you need to do is go to the title office, pay the fee to transfer the title to your name, sell or refinance, then pay another fee and transfer the title back to the trust. All of these steps can be an inconvenience and all will definitely cost you a little more money, but the peace of mind you gain will be well worth the financial cost.

Marianne

"My husband and I keep everything completely separate financially, even going so far as to file separate tax returns. It does cost us more, but at least I'm assured that everything I've worked so hard to accumulate stays out of the grasp of his ex. We keep separate bank accounts, but also have a power of attorney on each other. I also put my house in a trust when we married, so if anything happens to me, there is no way that my husband's ex-wife could get her hands on it."

Julia

"Financially, we keep everything separate. My husband didn't have much in the way of assets after the divorce anyway. All assets purchased since our marriage are in my name. Even in my will, my husband is left nothing. I know it sounds cold, but this is the only way we can ensure a little bit of financial stability."

This is sound advice. One second wife went through a living hell on earth because the State of Massachusetts seized her and her husband's joint checking account. Her husband was behind on support because he had been laid off from his job. If he would have paid the $275.00 per week as ordered, he and his present family of five would have been left with $50.00 per week. He stopped making child support payments so that he and his current family could survive. He filed papers with the court to cut his payments legally, but it took over five months before he could get a court date.

After enduring so much stress that she suffered a breakdown and was hospitalized, this second wife sued the State of Massachusetts (*Laubinger* v. *Massachusetts Dept. of Revenue/Child Support Enforcement*, Massachusetts Appeals Court 95-P-1441). Originally, the Massachusetts Attorney General said that it was legal to take the money from a joint account, even if the money belonged to only one of the account holders. The Massachusetts Appeals Court did not agree and after four years the State was ordered to return the money, along with a large amount of interest.

Although this second wife won this individual battle, her war continues. The government was granted qualified immunity, thus not being forced to face charges of violating due process. The government was also granted immunity for causing the enormous stress suffered by her, thereby escaping responsibility for her hospital bills, which have exceeded $20,000. This is a prime example of what our government, goaded by a psycho-bitch-ex-wife-from-hell, is capable of doing to innocent people trying to survive, keep a roof over their heads, and provide for their children the best they can. In the long run, it is well worth the cost, time, and inconvenience of keeping all accounts, moneys, and assets separate.

Jonie

"I went so far as to legally divorce my husband yet I continued to live with him. Sound strange? My husband owed back support which he was unable to pay because he lost his job. The ex-wife-from-hell convinced the courts to seize various assets belonging to him. Our family was left virtually penniless.

"I filed for welfare benefits, but was ineligible because I was married. After divorcing my husband, but still living with him, I and my children were eligible to receive cash benefits, medical coverage, and food stamps. It enabled the family to survive. The irony of all this is the fact that what I did was not illegal. It is just another example of the lack of logic in our present government. Eventually, my husband and I plan to remarry, on the same date as we were originally married."

Another second wife, in order to help her family cope with financial difficulties, developed a web site based on the universal demand for personalized Christmas gifts.

It's added work, but it's hers alone and it helps. All of the legal fees, child support, and spousal support have cost this couple a small fortune, but they're still together and working hard, loving and caring for each other. Check out the web site at http://www.centrinet.com/genie.htm. Their e-mail address is Christmas@centrinet.com.

Although not all second wives are mothers or stepmothers, all second wives do share the struggle to overcome the prejudiced perspective that most people have towards second wives. Even though millions of women are second wives, the image is still that of a home-wrecker, a trophy, or a stupid bimbo. This image problem is something that we are aware of, but it is not something that we should be ashamed of or even ignore. It is something that we can work together to change.

Second marriages have been referred to as the triumph of hope over experience. Despite one unfavorable encounter in the realm of love and marriage, your husband managed to maintain his optimism for a warm, loving relationship. In spite of his apprehension, he took another chance with you. You are the one and only person he can love, trust, and confide in. You are the true love of his life.

You, on the other hand, overcame your anxiety of marrying a divorcé despite any misgivings you might have had. The love you felt for your husband was your sole motivation. Maybe your husband made a few mistakes in his first marriage. That's okay. None of us is perfect, by any means. We all make mistakes. It's what we learn from these mistakes that's important. Your husband learned a lot from his first marriage. He experienced a lousy marriage, with an overabundance of personal conflict, and knows exactly what he wants from his relationship with you. He wants a warm, loving relationship with the woman he loves and he doesn't need anyone else's approval.

You and he, and your children if you have any, face complicated problems and challenges that most of the other married couples in the world will never encounter. Your love for each other can and will see you both through it all.

When you sit down together over a glass of wine and just talk about your love, you will find that relaxing in this way is a great inspiration. You have something that a lot of other women will never have. You have a husband who loves you more than anything else in the world. The two of you have the ability to establish a happy, loving family life for yourselves. Your love is something to be treasured and is worth more than anything money could buy. Guard it well, treasure it, and nurture it. Someday, the benefits will far outweigh the difficulties.

3

~*Psycho-Bitch-from-Hell*~

Vindictive, spiteful, manipulative, greedy, deceitful, lazy, vengeful, crass, bitter, hostile, vicious, ill-tempered, malicious, selfish, cunning, hypocritical, sanctimonious, vile, nasty, antagonistic, indolent, obstinate, deceptive, insincere, depraved, controlling, callous, unreasonable, irrational, illogical, inconsistent, insidious, contrary, heartless, inane, cold-blooded, cruel, barbaric, ugly, bloodthirsty, scathing, savage, irresponsible, hateful, disagreeable, crude, insane, psychotic, schizophrenic, and downright bitchy. Sound like anyone you know? You have probably used each and every one of these words to describe your husband's ex-wife at one time or another. Most second wives have to deal with one: It's the ex-wife-from-hell!

I'm not saying that every ex-wife is a bitch from hell. Far from it. There are some ex-wives who manage to put their personal feelings aside for the sake of the children. Yes, there are some ex-wives out there who understand and acknowledge that, for whatever reason, the marriage just didn't work.

Indeed, there are also numerous ex-wives who do not receive the support that they deserve for their children because, if the truth be told, there are men out there who don't pull their weight as parents. We know about them and we've all heard their stories. These women have valid complaints, but they are not the ex-wives that we are talking about here. In fact, most mothers who receive no child support are too busy working and trying to pay the rent to have time to think about torturing their ex-husbands and second wives.

The ex-wife-from-hell is not an abandoned welfare mother receiving no support whatsoever from a deadbeat dad who doesn't give a damn about his children. The ex-wife-from-hell is a bitch who uses the system to her own greedy advantage. Deadbeat dads have received a lot of publicity in recent years and the ex-wife-from-hell knows that the courts' sympathy always lies with the divorced mother. She has no problem twisting the laws that were meant to protect women into a torture rack for you and your husband.

The ex-wife-from-hell is a bitch who receives child support—a lot, on time, each and every month. The ex-wife-from-hell is a bitch who really doesn't care about the welfare of her children. She doesn't have time to get a job. She's too busy getting her hair and nails done. The ex-wife-from-hell has so much time on her hands, in fact, that she has nothing better to do other than think of ways to make her ex-husband's life miserable. She can afford to go to court any damn time she wants to, using her ex-husband's money. She loves to go to court and she does so frequently.

The ex-wife-from-hell cannot accept the fact that her ex-husband has moved on; she's rooted in the past. She's determined to make your life, your husband's life, and your stepchildren's lives absolutely miserable. You may wonder to yourself, "What was he thinking when he married this woman?" Maybe he was doing his thinking with his little head instead of his big head but, at this point, that's irrelevant. It's all in the past.

The important thing is the impact she will have on your life and your marriage. If you have been married and divorced yourself, you understand the powerful effect that divorce can have on your life. If this is your first marriage then there may be issues regarding divorce with which you may wish to familiarize yourself.

There are two aspects to divorce: the *legal* divorce and the *real* divorce. If you disregard the financial costs involved, the legal divorce is the easy one. A legal divorce gives a person a piece of paper which specifically spells out: a) the dissolution of the marriage; b) the division of marital property; c) the custodial arrangements for the children (if any); d) the child support payments, who makes the payments and how much; e) visitation periods for the noncustodial parent; and f) spousal support, if required.

The *real* divorce is the difficult one. The real divorce involves breaking off emotionally from a former partner. The real divorce is where most problems develop, problems that can affect a person for the remainder of his or her life. If your husband's ex-wife has never gotten her real divorce, she's still emotionally involved with your husband.

It doesn't matter who filed for divorce or even the reason for the divorce. If love weren't involved, getting a divorce would be just like dissolving any other type of business relationship and it wouldn't be such an emotional issue. If your husband's ex is the one who filed for divorce, she could be feeling guilty. She could be feeling angry with herself. She could be feeling lonely. She might even regret walking out on him and be wallowing in self-pity this very minute. If it was your husband who filed for divorce, his ex probably feels as if she was abandoned. She could be one of those ex-wives who claims to have "given x-number of years of her life to him." As if his life wasn't going on at the same time!

Emotions are involved. Hurt feelings can cause even the most rational, reasonable person to lose perspective.

Just think what these feelings can do to a person who might not be playing with a full deck! What can these feeling do to a person who is angry, petty, greedy, and mean-spirited to begin with, which might be part of the reason why her marriage failed in the first place.

Attitudes change. Personalities change. A person's whole outlook on life can change. A natural reaction to being hurt is to think of ways to hurt back, especially if we've been hurt by someone we love. Her desire for revenge, retaliation, and retribution can wreak havoc on your life for years to come.

This is where you really come into it. Maybe you met your husband when he was still married to his wife. Maybe you met him while he was in the middle of his divorce. Maybe you met him several years after his divorce was final. It really doesn't matter when or how you met him. If you're happy together, his ex-wife will hate you and probably blame you for the divorce. If his ex-wife is still involved emotionally with your husband, if she never got her *real* divorce, you have a serious problem, one that may not go away for years—maybe not ever.

Lee

"All the lawyers said that she would settle, but we knew from the outset that this woman would never settle. She wanted the court battle to go on forever, and it did—for twelve years."

Laura

"It is not the second or third wives who cause all the problems. It is that an ex-wife cannot bear the fact that her former husband is happy and she is so miserable taking care of the children she wanted custody of. Usually these are the women who divorced their husbands in the first place. Her attitude is that she did not want him, and by God, no one else is going to have him either. She has interfered with and disrupted our lives so many times and so badly, I can't even count."

Gloria

"I am sick of her still trying to control my fiancé in every little way possible, all the while proclaiming she is just the happiest person on earth. If she really were so damn happy, you would think she'd have better things to do than to try to make our lives a living hell!"

As most second wives know, custody issues are a favorite revenge-getting feeding ground for vindictive ex-wives. Most divorce decrees grant time periods in which the noncustodial parent (the father) is allowed to see his children. These time periods are usually quite specific, such as every other weekend, alternating holidays, or maybe four to six weeks in the summer. That's assuming that the kids still live within visiting distance.

If the ex-wife decides to move 3,000 miles away and takes the kids with her (because she has custody), then visitation can get a little more complicated, not to mention a lot more expensive. It's hard to see the kids every other weekend if you're living in New York and the ex-wife and kids are living in California. If travel arrangements are involved, guess what? Your husband probably has to pay for those too. These arrangements are not conducive to a healthy relationship between the children and their father.

How can your husband be involved in his children's lives when he has little or no contact with them? Who can possibly be a good father when he only sees his kids four days a month, sometimes only once a year? And that's only if the ex-wife-from-hell decides to *let* him see the kids. The ex-wife-from-hell who never got her *real* divorce gets her jollies from interfering in every way she can with the court-ordered visitation to which your husband is entitled. Court orders mean nothing to her.

Roberta

"In my husband's custody agreement, it plainly states that he is to have visitation with the children every other Christmas from the closure of school until 24 hours before school resumes. The ex was supposed to inform him of the dates involved. Of course, she didn't, so this year we contacted the school in early November, got the dates, and bought the plane tickets. The children were scheduled to leave two days after school got out. Well, my husband talked to the kids and my stepdaughter informed him that she has a playoff game a couple of days before Christmas. Surprise, surprise, the ex didn't even inform my husband of the possibility of this happening. She knew that the kids were to come stay with us this Christmas. Now my stepdaughter is all upset about this and wants us to switch the dates. This is impossible because the tickets are non-refundable. This is just one in a long line of problems that the ex has caused because she is too immature to put the best interests of her children in front of her own sick compulsion to make life difficult for my husband."

Another thing that the ex-wife-from-hell uses to make your life miserable is child support. Kids are worth money, in the court's eye, and you better believe she plans on getting every red cent that she can for them. Not that any of this money will actually be used for the kids. Hell, no, she just wants to put you in the poorhouse. It's really disgusting to see the ex-wives demanding cash-under-the-table before they "allow" the visit. Selling children to their own fathers? It won't make the six o'clock news, you can be sure of that.

Sally

"When my husband and I met, he was paying $400 per month in child support for the two children from his first marriage. As soon as we moved to California (to be closer to the kids, of course) and my husband started to work for his original employer, his ex filed for an increase in child support. The court then ordered a payment of $700 per month. The court took into consideration 15 percent of *my* income as well. The ex-wife does not work and her new hubby earns about $80,000 per year. Now one of the children has turned 18 and, with the California child support guidelines the way they are, it looks as if we'll still be paying $700-$800 per month for one child!"

Liza

"My spouse's ex worked at home, did not claim all of her income, therefore, my spouse paid more for one child than what I received for two. His ex stopped paying on the debts she was responsible for in the divorce decree. Then the court began to garnish his pay! Creditors could not get payment from her as she was self-employed and lied about her income. The bankruptcy court decided that since I was working, making a fairly decent living, as well as receiving child support, that I could easily support the family. All of my husband's income was designated to go to his ex and to pay her bills. Basically, she was going to live a comfortable life-style at the expense of me and my family. I received a note from the ex after all this was over stating, 'You should never have taken him from me. I never stopped loving him even after I divorced him. If I can't have him, neither will you, and you will pay.' "

Janice

"My husband pays nearly $400 per month on a minimum wage job. She repeatedly denies visitation or refuses to meet him halfway, as specifically spelled out in the divorce papers. She has new furniture, two new TV's, and is on her fourth live-in boyfriend. Do you really think she'll go to jail for being in contempt by denying visitation? I don't think so. But you can sure bet that if my husband misses just one payment, his ass will be in jail."

Nancy

"When you marry a man with kids, you also marry his ex. She'll always be their mother and she will never go away. Before you marry, you need to decide if you can live with the knowledge that, for the next five to ten to eighteen years (depending on the ages of his children), you will be giving her (and her kids) as much as half of your money. She will have and you will do without."

Rita

"I've helped my fiancé with every one of his court petitions. He got screwed because the judge hates men and temporary guidelines do not take into consideration the realities of life. If I didn't have a job and wasn't paying for our housing, our food, and everything else, he would be out sleeping on the street. I resent having to finance his ex-wife's manicures and vacations."

The ex-wife-from-hell is not above making false accusations of abuse, physical or sexual. Actually, we can blame the lawyers for this, often as not, because many of them recommend an accusation of abuse, real or not, to get an advantage in a custody battle. And once the abuse ball gets rolling, an ex-wife-from-hell can have a field day with the leverage it gives her.

Darla

"My husband's ex swore under oath that he abused her and that was all it took to make him look like a criminal in the eyes of the law. The wheels of injustice rolled right over him."

Needless to say, these are real-life examples of what second wives endure every day. Regardless of economic status, second wives cope and cope and cope with ex-wives-from-hell who have all the ammunition they need. A vindictive ex-wife-from-hell, who never got her *real* divorce and who can't stand the fact that her ex-husband has gone on with his life, will go to any extent to cause trouble in your marriage. She will hurt her own children, just to hurt your husband. She poisons the children's minds against their father and against you as well. She lies to the kids, manipulates them, and puts them on guilt trips. You have no control over what she does and you cannot change her.

The one and only thing that you can control is your reaction to her, and a reaction from you is exactly what she wants. Your job is to believe in yourself, in your husband, and in your marriage. Remember, she is the one who is all fucked up, not you!

Angel

"I had never seen anyone so malicious as Bill's ex-wife. She would call Bill and invite him out to dinner on the pretense of discussing some problems with the kids. Sometimes she would just call and want to just chat with Bill. She would send messages with the kids when they came to visit, things like, 'Mom was talking about all the fun the two of you had on that vacation to Florida and wanted us to ask you if you remember.' If I answered the telephone, she would say things like, 'you bitch,' and hang up, as if I didn't recognize her voice. An answering machine and caller ID has been a godsend to us. I don't even answer the phone if it's her. If she leaves a message, fine. She was the one who had the affair. Now she's alone and lonely. Oh, well. Bill and I are a team. He's a great guy and I can't help it if she was too stupid and self-centered to realize what a catch she had. Her feminine wiles don't work like they used to when she was younger and she can't stand it. As far as I'm concerned, she doesn't even exist."

Stacy

"I used to get so upset when Jimmy's ex would call. They don't even have any kids, so what the hell was she calling him for? Jimmy was so patient with me, constantly reassuring me that he loved me and that I had nothing to worry about. He told me she wasn't worth the aggravation. He would politely ask her what she wanted, explain to her that there was nothing more to discuss (and there wasn't, everything had been covered in the divorce papers), and hang up.

"She kept at it for almost six months until she realized she couldn't tear us apart or get Jimmy back. It was a matter of my trusting my husband and ignoring some stupid, petty, jealous woman who couldn't get over the fact that she lost the best thing she ever had."

This might sound sarcastic, but John Lennon once said, "It's really lawyers that make divorces nasty. You know, if there was a nice ceremony like a wedding for a divorce, it'd be much better." I have to agree with him. Consider this concept for just a minute. With so many divorces nowadays, if we haven't been divorced ourselves, we probably know someone who has. A ceremony is basically a symbol of a life change—a rite of passage—made public. It's an announcement to the world that a transformation has taken place. These ceremonies play an important role in our lives, the baptisms, the wedding ceremonies, the bar and bat mitzvahs, and even the funeral services. Each ritual has its own special significance, acknowledging that a change has occurred.

Divorce is certainly a rite of passage, a total and complete transformation of a former life. Maybe having a ceremony would help speed up the healing process for the ex-wife-from-hell. She could be the center of attention, which is exactly what she wants. Her family and friends could gather and offer condolences. The change in her life could be acknowledged by all the people who are important to her. Maybe the ceremony would help the ex-wife-from-hell, who never got her *real* divorce, to finally understand that the relationship is over. It might help her realize that she has run out of chances to correct her many mistakes.

Maybe such a ceremony would have consoled one particular ex-wife in North Carolina enough so that she could get on with her life. She claimed that she and her husband were happily married and had the perfect storybook marriage until another woman came along and stole her husband from her. What a crock! If a couple is in love and happy in their relationship, nobody can come along and steal anybody from anybody else. Grow up.

Only a handful of states still recognize "alienation of affection" suits which date back to the eighteenth century when women were still considered property. According to *Time* (August 18, 1997), this particular ex-wife actually convinced a jury to rule in her favor and was awarded a one million dollar settlement to be paid by the second wife! The subtext here for second wives is: Be on alert! This is how angry society can get at you for daring to exist. Courts will even reach back a hundred years to find a law to punish you.

Of course, they change the law to suit themselves. So, it is not okay for a husband to own his wife, but it *is* okay for a wife to own her husband, a little turnaround that was never pointed out in any of the media coverage. In my opinion, if she had put as much effort into her marriage as she did into her vindictive lawsuit, she wouldn't be crying in her pretzels today. After all, if you and your husband haven't been intimate in several years and he sleeps on the couch, do you need to be smacked upside the head with a two-by-four to realize that something is wrong with your relationship?

From her appearance on *Dateline NBC* (December 15, 1997), the whole country learned that this ex-wife receives a whopping $4,000 each month for alimony and child support. That's $48,000 per year, a lot more money than many two-income families earn, so what the hell is her problem anyway? Talk about a poor loser. Ain't life a bitch!

The second wife in this scenario, a discerning individual, bears no malice to this vindictive dumped wife. During the *Dateline* show, she said of her husband's ex-wife, "Until she can acknowledge that she shares in the responsibility of the breakdown of that marriage, she can never get on with her life."

Hallelujah to that!

4

~The Wicked Stepmother~

The overall perception of stepmothers is that they are evil, hateful second wives who find sheer pleasure in making the lives of their stepchildren a living hell. This viewpoint traces its roots to fairy tales such as *Cinderella, Snow White,* and *Hansel and Gretel.* Originally, fairy tales were simple entertaining ways of passing along knowledge to the young. While they worked at mundane and boring tasks such as cooking, cleaning, and sewing, women entertained each other and their children by telling stories. These stories were often reflections of their lives at the time.

Up until the twentieth century, the stepmother was a rare creature, although not totally unknown. People didn't get divorced often. Most men only remarried if the first wife died. Before the no-fault divorce laws, many people stayed married, even if they were miserable, due to the costs and the trauma of proving fault.

Change brought us new situations, arrangements, and possibilities. Families struggled to put together groups of people not previously related. Often these families were troubled, helplessly feeling their way through unknown territory.

The survival of any species is based on the natural love of parents towards their children and the natural instinct toward procreation and protection of the young. In the animal world, it's highly unusual to find a stepmother. We hear, from time to time, of the mother cat who nurtures a stray or of a wolf raising a human child. Mostly, however, this is the stuff of myth.

The natural reaction of most animals is to let a motherless newborn die, if not to eat it. It is simply not an instinctive behavior, either for animals or for people, to love and care for a young one other than your own. I'm not saying it can't be done, but it is difficult to do.

Who can blame a woman for struggling to love the offspring of a woman she hates? Witness the difficulties often encountered by willing adoptive parents. This bond, tenuous at best, cannot always be expected to be a strong one, certainly not as strong as the natural bond of mother to child. And yet, in spite of stereotypes, second wives these days do an unappreciated great job of nurturing their stepchildren.

Every stepmother today recognizes the stereotype, the bias, and the bold hostility towards stepmothers. They deal with it every day.

"Oh, you're not her real mother?"

"I didn't know John had remarried."

"How do the children cope with you?"

People can really be stupid, can't they? As if it's any of their damn business or as if they really care. You know it's not worth getting upset over, but sometimes all the stupidity just gets to you.

It's okay to let it get to you, but it's not okay to let anyone know it. When somebody says something stupid, let it go. Don't feed into their stupidity. No matter how mad you are, take a deep breath and smile. Then go ahead and have some fun. Be catty. Pretend you can't read between the lines. As long as you keep on smiling, you can get away with saying something stupid right back:

"You mean to tell me John's ex didn't call you? I'm so surprised. She called everyone else in town as soon as the divorce was final."

You're going to run into stupid people everywhere. Who really cares if you offend them? They certainly have no qualms about being rude or offensive, so fuck them. You have your own priorities, and your family is number one on the list.

Raising kids is always a challenge. They can be a real pain in the ass, whether they're your biokids or your stepkids. You love your stepchildren, even if they annoy, aggravate, or just plain piss you off at times. You love them because they're a part of the man you love. You notice the way different elements of his personality surface in each child. You're aware of the bond between father and child and you're going to do all you can to facilitate that bond. You might even create one of your own.

Intellectually, you understand that your stepkids had nothing to do with the breakup of their parents' marriage. They deserve the chance to just be kids and have happy childhoods. Emotionally, however, it's a different story.

Sara

"I used to think of them and treat them just as my own biokids. When their mother interfered with the visitation, I fought with their mother. I have since backed off and I let their father deal with all of it. I treat them politely and considerately, but I don't put my heart and soul into it like I used to. I truly love them, but I love myself too, and I am tired of being hurt by them."

The difficulties can increase if you have your own children from a prior marriage. If your children live with you and your husband (the most likely situation), they have to share your time and attention with stepbrothers and sisters at a time when they may still be feeling the effects of your divorce. They have to adjust to a stepfather, whose personality may be totally different from their father. Depending upon the number of children involved, your family's income, and the size of your house, they may even have to share rooms with kids they don't even like!

Disciplining two sets of kids who may be used to different methods is a serious undertaking—one that could drive you to an early grave. At least you know your own kids. You've been there since day one. You've always been the authority figure in their eyes. You know what works and what doesn't work. Not so with your stepkids. They may resent you "trying to take their mother's place," and might, themselves, still be recovering from the divorce. These considerations can render them less than cooperative.

If your husband hesitates to discipline his kids for fear of losing them, he sure as hell isn't going to jump right in and help you discipline your own kids. It's tough to tell someone else's children how to behave, even if they are in your house. What if they don't comply? They know exactly the degree to which your hands are tied.

Things could actually get to the point where you resent your stepchildren. You could begin to view your weekend visitors as nothing more than intruders, those little imps who show up every other weekend and whose only objective in life is to make your life miserable. You might even get to the point of resenting your husband. These feelings are not conducive to a healthy, happy marriage. They are common feelings, however, and are symptomatic of the normal frustrations in dealing with the dynamics of a stepfamily.

Cheryl

"The kids want to visit, but they don't want to help. They think of themselves as guests. My point is, regardless of whether you're here two days, two weeks, or two months, I am not your servant and the world does not revolve around you. There are no rules at their bio-mother's house; they have no responsibilities. Their rooms are a mess. Their mom doesn't care at all."

Gail

"I used to get so upset every other weekend when Tom's kids would come visit. They were rude; they refused to help do any chores whatsoever. After a couple of months and many tears on my part, I had a long talk with Tom. I told him I understood how important his kids were to him, but if things didn't change, eventually he'd have his kids but not me. We sat down with the kids on their next visit, explained to them that even though we only saw each other every other weekend, we were still a family and that we have certain rules. I wasn't sure what their reactions were going to be but it was as if they were waiting for us to take control. Things have gone great since then."

You, as a second wife and stepmother, must deal with your stepchildren's pain, anger, resentment, alienation, hatred, and disrespectful attitudes. All of these emotions might be directed towards either you or your husband. And if your husband's ex-wife happens to be immature and vindictive, it only makes matters worse.

Remember, the children are not responsible for the situation. They're caught in the middle and are trying to survive the best that they can. They are not adults and they do not understand the finality of divorce. Many times, the kids think that the situation is only temporary. The kids might realize that their mom and dad have had problems, but they are unable to understand the seriousness of the situation. Deep down inside, regardless of their ages, they are probably hoping that their parents will eventually get back together.

Sharon

"This morning I went into my stepdaughters' room and saw a picture drawn by the younger girl. It was a picture of her 'family.' The picture consisted of her, her sister, their mother, and their father. I understand the fact that most children dream of the day when their parents will get back together, but does it ever end? I mean, after both parents remarry, and they aren't little kids anymore, does it ever end?"

Cris

"My stepson feels that since I am not his mother, he does not have to listen to me. Since his father basically backed him on this concept until recently, I have a hard fight ahead of me to gain the respect that I know I deserve. My stepson maintains that he hates his mother, who has done many emotionally scarring things to him. However, he constantly tries to reach out to her to gain her acceptance and love, even though she can't see this. I, on the other hand, am the person who cares for him on a daily basis, doing nice things for him, paying for everything, and almost literally bending over backwards for him. And I am still considered a bitch in his eyes."

Marjorie

"Lately, my husband's ex has told the kids that they do not have to listen to me and criticizes me to them. They, like kids, would love the opportunity to not have to listen to an adult and have responded by not listening to me. She has also told them that they can call her anytime they are with us, 'if they have a problem,' and she will come get them. Of course, their only 'problem' is not getting their way."

If the children's mother is an emotional basket case, irrational and destructive, she's probably driving her own children crazy at home. You know that she's interfering with your husband's visitation and poisoning her children's minds against their father and you. You can only imagine the scene at her place.

When they're with you and their father, they need to experience a home with rules and stability that is run by mature, reasonable adults. Someone has to teach them what life is all about. It's a parental responsibility. If nobody ever teaches kids how to behave with proper manners, how to clean up after themselves, or how to interact with people in a respectable way, the consequences are detrimental to all concerned. It might seem, at times, to be an overwhelming and thankless mission, but at least you will have a clear conscience knowing that you did your best, considering the circumstances.

Don't doubt yourself; it'll be worth it in the long run. When they're grown, the kids will remember that you were patient, reasonable, affectionate, and didn't bad-mouth their mother, even though she had nothing nice to say about you. They will realize that their mother lied, and she will lose her children's respect while you will have gained it. It ain't easy being a saint!

Jenny

"I grew up living with my mother and visiting my father and stepmother. Now that I'm an adult, I'd like other stepmothers to benefit from a few things that I learned as a child. First of all, your stepchildren aren't guests. They are family members. Every family has its own set of rules, codes, and ethics. These must be adhered to by each and every family member. If you don't teach your children and stepchildren to respect these rules and family boundaries, who will?

"There might be a period of time during which you suffer, because kids can definitely be jerks, but in the long run you will earn their respect."

Keeping these thoughts in mind as you deal with the everyday ups and downs might make things a little easier. Picture your stepkids fully grown, as successful and well-rounded adults, living a full and satisfying life—far, far away! Keep a running countdown calendar going (in your mind, of course). *Only 12 years and 4 months until she moves out. Only 9 years and 7 months until he leaves. Peace and quiet at last!*

As if it isn't difficult enough to deal with the events inside your own home, just wait until you step outside. You, as a stepmother, have absolutely no rights, as far as the courts are concerned, regarding your stepchildren. You can't even take your stepchildren to an emergency room if necessary and complete paperwork so that they can be treated. Nobody will care if the kid just broke his neck because he felt like playing Superman and fell off the roof. Nobody will care if the kid just ate fertilizer because her big brother dared her to do it. You are not their *real* mother so you have no biological relationship to these children. The hospital staff will not take you seriously, except when it comes to paying the bill. Then they'll be sure to ask you for your home address and insurance.

Be prepared to deal with emergencies ahead of time, just in case. Some stepmothers have their husbands write out a statement advising whomever it concerns that you are his wife and have his permission to authorize emergency medical care for his children. Why not make one up for yourself this week? Put it in a safe place, just in case. It should be dated, signed, and notarized.

Of course, a trip to the hospital emergency room is never as frightening as a trip to court. That will scare the hell out of any second wife. What is she after now? What else is there to take? Can we endure this again? Inevitably, the kids will get dragged into it. So do your best to explain the situation to your stepchildren in such a way that they don't feel their security is threatened.

Depending upon the children's ages, more or less information can be given. Little kids don't really need to be bombarded with arguments over mortgage payments, taxes, or even private school tuition. If this is purely an exercise in torture for your husband's ex-wife, you may have to bite your tongue sometimes. Regardless of your own feelings, you must not bad-mouth their mother in front of them.

Remember, you are a mature adult whose only desire is to be an excellent mother to all of your kids, whether they're your natural children or your stepchildren. They will learn from you how to deal with conflict in a responsible and mature way which, in the long run, will benefit your entire family. You will also end up with a clear conscience, as well as the respect of your family.

If you're a second wife and stepmother who deeply loves her husband and family—biokids *and* stepkids—but is feeling overwhelmed by the difficulties you face, you are not alone. Being a mother is a tough job, probably the toughest in the world. Everything you say and do has an impact on your children. Their personalities, thoughts, and feelings are a direct reflection of your influence. Being a stepmother is even tougher, especially if the biological mother is constantly interfering. If you're both a mother and a stepmother trying to blend two different families into one, you deserve a medal.

You have probably faced the reality of the situation by now. You experience heartaches, headaches, migraines, maybe even high blood pressure, ulcers, and more than a few gray hairs. People talk behind your back. It comes with the territory. You're torn in a million different directions everyday and you probably feel like no one knows what you go through.

But you are wrong. Millions of women are second wives and millions of women are going through situations very much like yours. We deserve respect for what we endure and for what we contribute to society. Let's face it, most of us take screwed-up, hurt, and troubled children, born of women we hate, and make them whole again.

We save their kids for them! Damn right, we deserve a medal and more. We deserve a little peace of mind, and maybe a fur coat or a trip to Europe . . . .

5

~Considering the Kids~

The real victims in any divorce are the children. They're caught between a rock and a hard place. They love their mothers. They love their fathers. Divorce has shattered their lives. The world as they've known it has gone down the toilet with one quick flush. Some adults who get divorced are hard pressed to say what went wrong or when it went wrong. Many knew they shouldn't have gotten into the situation in the first place, but they didn't pay attention to those little voices in their heads. Whatever the reason, everyone suffers the consequences which are costly, both financially and emotionally. It takes years for adults to recover from divorce. Imagine how the kids feel! They didn't even have a choice in the matter.

Why did Daddy go away? Why can't Daddy come home? When will we see Daddy? Where is Daddy? Why are you so mad, Mommy? How come I can't call Daddy and talk to him? How come we only get to see Daddy every two weeks? I miss my Daddy. Why did you leave us, Daddy? Don't you love us anymore?

It's normal for kids to ask these questions. The answers given to these questions will affect them for the rest of their lives. Parents entangled in their own emotions are often incapable of coping with their kids' feelings. How can they possibly help someone else when they can't even help themselves?

Your stepkids' emotional problems probably began long before you entered into the picture. It doesn't matter one damn bit. These kids are caught up in the aftermath of a great battle and you're stuck cleaning up the mess. If your husband's ex-wife has custody of the children, this means that your husband has no rights whatsoever concerning his children. None. Zero. *Zilch.* The children must learn to adapt to an ever-changing life-style, contingent upon the whims of their mother at any given moment, all at a time when what they need most is some stability in their lives. You have no rights either, nor do you have any say-so in the way the children are raised, at least in the eyes of the law.

Jan

"The only rights you have are those your husband allows you to have, and then it's only when the children are with you. Step-mothering is a tough pill to swallow, and sometimes, if there is a large geographical distance to cover and infrequent visitation, you must realize that there is only so much you can do during your and your husband's absences from their lives. I'm not saying you should give up trying, but their mother can put up brick walls, and the only thing you will accomplish is to drive yourself crazy."

Those weekend visitors in your life have a way of disrupting an otherwise peaceful life-style, don't they? Little reminders of your husband's former life with *her*.

Jane

"How do you put up with the rotten behavior of a child that you didn't bring into this world? How do you have someone running around that your significant other cherishes more than his life and you didn't have anything to do with? How do you discipline your child for doing something to the other child? How do you force yourself to stay up all night caring for a sick child, cleaning up her vomit, taking her temperature, having her spit up medicine at you, when your own kids are sound asleep in their beds? Being a mother to begin with scared me half to death. Trying to be a mother to another woman's child makes me question my sanity at times."

When it comes to stepchildren, your open, honest communication with your husband is the most important key to the survival of your marriage. Discussing how you feel about your husband's children may not be easy, but it is necessary. Sit down with him and voice your concerns and feelings. He may share them!

Jane

"Don't get me wrong. I love the kids, but I wasn't ready to be a mom. All my husband did was add to my confusion. Because I married him, I became an instant parent. This was not what I signed up for. He can't understand that there is something that isn't there, that will never, ever be there. How can I pretend to be something that I will never be?"

Linda

"Having no children of my own when I became a stepmother ten years ago, I was totally unprepared not only for being a parent, but for all the feelings of confusion and self-doubt. I was not prepared to deal with the intense interpersonal dynamics, the responsibility, and expectations put on me by both my husband and myself."

These feelings are perfectly normal, especially if you have no children of your own. You didn't have nine months to get used to the idea of motherhood. Moreover, this is not really your child! You love the father, to be sure, but you can probably see the mother's image in the child's little face and sometimes it's a difficult sight to bear. To be thrust into instant motherhood, expected to care for and love someone else's children, is something of an unnatural and difficult job, especially when it's only part-time.

Francesca

"I had two children from a previous marriage when I met Eddie. He had also been married before and had two children as well. Most mothers will be the first to admit that there are days when they just cannot stand their kids, no matter how much they love them. Kids get on your nerves. That's just the way it is. Acknowledging this fact is hard for many people, but it's true, nonetheless. Trying to explain to your husband that you just can't stand his kids is a difficult thing to do. There were times I just had to bite my tongue."

Carol

"Being a teacher and dealing with kids all day long, it was a little easier for me when I tried to explain to my husband exactly *how* kids can get to you, especially after being with them all day long. We made an arrangement that we would take turns being the person who was responsible to care for *all* the children's needs and wants, and after doing that only a couple of times, he realized just how demanding and tiring caring for children can be."

Try to look at the situation from your husband's perspective, especially if he is the noncustodial parent. His visitation with his kids is minimal, at best. At least he's in there, fighting to be a father to his kids. Not all men bother to do so when the going gets rough.

Your husband loves his children, and he pays his child support and spends as much time with them as he can. Think of how devoted he'll be to any children that you and he might have together.

Kelly

"I tried to make the weekends that the stepchildren *weren't* visiting special. Every other Saturday night, we would both fix a new recipe, open a bottle of wine, and have a candlelight dinner. We played music and danced after dinner. Sometimes we stayed up until three in the morning."

Natalie

"On our 'off' weekends, we don't have to worry about kids waking us up early on Sunday morning. So sometimes I bring out the sexy lingerie and we have time to get as wild as we want to before the day begins."

Pamela

"It's hard enough on a day-to-day basis to deal with all the bullshit. The weekends without kids were our chance to be a *couple*. We went out to dinner. Sometimes we stayed home and had a candlelight dinner. If we felt like going to a nightclub, we went out. If we wanted to stay home, watch a movie, get cozy, then that's what we did. It was like being a teenager all over again."

On its own and by itself, being a stepmother is not easy. Add to it, however, an ex-wife-from-hell and your role seems to get more stressful and difficult every day. Some of these ex-wives, not caring about the welfare of their own children, have gone to extremes, using their children as pawns to hurt their ex-husbands. These women simply do not care about the damage that they inflict on the kids. They are hurting their ex-husbands and you to be sure, but they are hurting their children even more.

Kids aren't prepared to deal with the mind games played with them, especially by one of their parents and, as a result, they suffer far more than they should. Parental Alienation Syndrome is a condition that may develop in children whose parents are or have been involved in a bitter custody battle. In this condition, a child develops an obsessive, irrational hatred of the parent without custody (usually the father, in 95 percent of divorces). The custodial parent, the mother who never got her *real* divorce, alienates the child from the father out of spite. These tactics vary, as do the results, depending upon the emotional state of the mother as well as the vulnerability of the child.

In a mild form of Parental Alienation Syndrome, the custodial parent simply uses subtle tactics, such as telling the child, "Visitation is your choice. I won't force you to go, if you don't want to go." The custodial mother does nothing to encourage visits between the child and father, nor does she express any concern over missed visits. She does not promote any sort of communication between visits. Often she does not acknowledge or alleviate any distress that the child might be feeling due to loss of contact with the father.

Deep down, the mother might recognize that the father plays a significant role in his child's life, but due to her own unresolved emotional issues, she is unable to encourage the child's relationship with the father. She communicates her dislike of the visitation with statements such as, "You can see your father, but you know how much I don't like it when you go there." The mother might refuse to listen to anything that the child might have to say about the other parent. "I don't want to hear about what you did while you were with your father. I simply don't want to know." The mother might make negative comments about the father to the child, such as, "The divorce is all your father's fault, you know. Your father doesn't love you or he wouldn't have left us." Through statements made and not made, the mother places all the blame for the divorce on the father, at least in the child's eyes.

Moreover, the mother might place all blame for any financial problems on the father, in order to further alienate father and child. The psycho ex-wife-from-hell might say things such as, "We wouldn't be broke if it weren't for him. He doesn't pay child support (or enough child support). He has a new wife to support and doesn't care if we starve to death or have a place to live. She's more important than you now. He doesn't love you anymore." Or she might make the child feel guilty for wanting to spend time with the father by saying, "I'm so lonely when you go to your father's house. You know, I miss you when you're gone. There's nothing for me to do."

In reality, this kind of behavior on the part of the mother becomes a twisted form of survival for the child. He might be unable to handle the separation. By connecting to the mother's anger, the child focuses on it and it gives him something concrete to hate and blame—the father.

All this anger and hatred is now directly aimed at your husband. The mother who has never gotten her *real* divorce is using her child's instinctive love as a weapon against her ex-husband, to her child's detriment. The child is too young and emotionally immature to understand the mother's manipulation.

Your husband's daughter is too young to understand the dual cause and blame of the divorce. All she knows is that Daddy's little girl doesn't have a daddy at home any longer. Daddy is a weekend treat or an obligation. Daddy's role has diminished so much that friends, neighbors, and even acquaintances may have more influence on her life than Daddy does.

For boys, a hideous mixture of anger at the father and protection of the mother turns a young heart into a flaming ball of rage. Naturally, this cannot be healthy for your husband's son and you might cringe as you watch him try to reconcile his anger and his love for his father during excruciating visits.

Janie

"My husband's ex-wife has spent the last eight years trying to turn the kids against their father. She moved constantly the first five years, so the kids had to attend five different schools in as many years. She filed papers with the court saying that my husband was behind in child support, which wasn't true. We had the canceled checks to prove that he wasn't behind in his payments, but it didn't make a damn bit of difference. The courts garnished his wages anyway. It took us two months to straighten that mess out.

"She's been married and divorced twice since she divorced my husband and has had children by both men. Of course, she's receiving child support from all three men. Consequently, she is receiving more money tax free in child support than I make working full-time. She doesn't work, but why should she? She even gets food stamps! She constantly tells the kids that their father is well-off and that she has no money, so every time the kids need or want something, her answer is, 'Go ask your father.'

"My husband says, 'What's the point in trying to maintain any normality in their lives or in mine? I think about them day and night. I pick up the phone a thousand times a day and put it back down. I envisioned spending quality time with my children. The reality is that I am no longer a part of their lives. I'm a visitor, nothing more. They're busy with their activities and many times on the weekends when I plan to pick them up, their activities interfere with my visitation. I can't bring myself to say, *No, You can't play baseball, I'm coming to pick you up.* I am watching them grow farther and farther away from me as all the other people in their lives try to take my place.'"

Most noncustodial fathers are familiar with such situations. They miss their children and their children miss them. Kids who grow up without fathers are missing an important piece out of their lives. It's heartbreaking, really.

Each child reacts differently, yet there are some basic similarities. Says Dr. Joan Kelly in her book, *Joint Custody and Shared Parenting*, "There is some evidence that in our well-meaning efforts to save children in the immediate post-separation period from anxiety, confusion, and the normative divorce-engendered conflict, we have set the stage in the longer run for the more ominous symptoms of anger, depression, and a deep sense of loss by depriving the child of the opportunity to maintain a full relationship with each parent."

If the results of your husband's divorce aren't this extreme, then the stress, anger, confusion, and insecurity that the children are feeling may manifest themselves in other ways—in their daily behavior. Some kids can't deal with these feelings in any other way. It's hard enough for adults to understand their emotions and to express them in socially acceptable ways. How can anyone expect kids to do the same, especially without someone to show them the way?

Children of divorce might have problems in school, at home, and socially. A polite child may turn defiant. A good student's grades might take a nosedive. The children might seek solace in questionable friendships or in socially unacceptable acts. Sometimes there is a complete change in personality. Symptoms vary with each child and not all are quite so severe. However, it's best to be prepared to deal with a multitude of behaviors.

Professional counselors and therapists all agree that, for the benefit of everyone concerned, divorced parents should put personal feelings aside and communicate with each other in a civil and responsible way. Mutual respect and consideration, with considerable significance placed upon the welfare of the children, should be the main priorities.

Excuse me while I puke. If the couple could have communicated effectively and respectfully with each other in the first place, they wouldn't be in the position they're in! Problems and disagreements would have been discussed calmly and rationally, and they would have been able to come to mutually agreed-upon resolutions for all the issues which eventually destroyed their marriage. They would have never gotten divorced. They would be living happily ever after, and I wouldn't be writing this book.

There are probably a few exceptionally rational and mature couples out there who agreed to divorce and can manage to be reasonable after their divorce, but they are obviously very few and far between! The divorce lawyers wouldn't be living on Park Avenue and the courtrooms wouldn't be bloody battle grounds if ex-wives could handle rejection. So much for counselors! Everybody turns to them for knee-jerk answers and that's what they get. Too bad it's usually a bunch of useless (but expensive) balony.

Children are nothing more than innocent victims of the war called divorce. Two people who once loved and cherished each other are now each other's worst enemy. Money, furniture, bank accounts, and kids become coveted possessions, to be divided as the spoils of war. Does it really benefit the children when the wife almost always wins every battle in this war? Wouldn't a more even-handed division be more beneficial to the children?

You'll need to develop your own arsenal of tactics to deal with the children of this war called divorce. First and foremost, you and your husband must reassure the children that they are not to blame for the divorce. Kids have a tendency to blame themselves and to feel that maybe if they had behaved better or listened more, their parents would still be together.

As parents, you must show the children that your love for them is absolutely and totally unconditional. Limits have to be set regarding behavior, but the children must understand that you love them in spite of their faults. They should feel safe and secure in your home. Even if, and especially if their mother is too immature or vindictive to overcome her personal feelings, your home must become a haven for them. Yes, in a sense, it *is* a competition, but the welfare of the children is at stake and that is far more important than your desire to rise above it all or to sidestep the whole problem. In fact, when it comes to creating a happy home, you will find yourself competing with her and probably winning.

Above all, you must keep the demands on a child in perspective. At his mother's house, the child might be expected to become the "man of the house." Kids have their childhoods to experience, and the mother's expectations and demands might be putting undue pressure on a child, or even on a teenager. Even if responsibilities increase after divorce, the children, both boys and girls, need to be left to their studies, their friends, and their childhood experiences as much as possible.

Your husband depends (even if unwillingly) on his ex-wife to care for his children on a day-to-day basis. Sure, you and he could do a better job, but often there is no choice. Therefore, your goal is not to make his children feel bad about their home or their mother. The better they feel about her, the better they will do in her charge.

So, do your best to encourage your stepchildren's relationship with their mother, even if you cannot stand the bitch. She is their mother and the children have a strong, natural bond with her. If their mother bad-mouths you to the children, let it go. It's not going to do you any good to get upset, nor is it going to do the children any good. You can find a place to rant and rave, if necessary, out of earshot of the kids. You can even buy a punching bag and get a workout in while you picture yourself beating the shit out of the woman. But, never, never, never let the kids see that anything that their mother says about you bothers you. You don't want to stoop to her level. Remember, you're the better woman.

You and your husband must listen to the kids, talk with them, and answer their questions honestly. Never lie to the kids about anything, regardless of the topic. The truth about the divorce and the breakdown of the relationship between parents can be explained simply, according to the age level of the kids. More details can eventually be told, as the children grow and mature. However, it is critical that you tell the them the truth, and tell it in a way that does not belittle or degrade either parent. Kids were born out of this relationship. The goal is to shield them from feeling terrible about the fact that their parents ever met and conceived them. No one wants to feel deep down that he or she was a mistake that never should have happened.

You want to do the best for your children and your stepchildren. It will be hard to achieve your ideals day in and day out. Your husband will probably cooperate, but you cannot expect this from his ex-wife. She might not give a rat's ass about the welfare of your stepchildren. She might dump the kids on you without a moment's notice because she wants a free babysitter. She might spread rumors about you all over town. She might threaten her children if they dare to like you.

You can only do so much. Kids deserve a chance to have at least one functional household, and your efforts to provide them with that, along with those of your husband, will pay off in the end. Ultimately, they will seek out the best place for their own comfort and development.

Several states have recently passed laws requiring divorcing parents to attend a class to understand the impact that divorce has on their children. When the class is completed, a certificate is issued and this certificate must be filed with the court before the divorce can proceed. The intent is to help parents understand that it's not the divorce itself which scars the children, it's the constant fighting after the divorce that traumatizes them.

Talk about hopeless! As if a class would have any impact on his ex whatsoever. If only she would take a few classes, maybe then she could get a job . . . uh, oh, watch out. There you go!

Your stepchildren probably bear the scars of a bitter divorce. They may still be hurting. One of the worst things that a child often feels is that he or she was the cause of the divorce. If your husband's ex-wife is a bitch from hell, playing mind games with the kids and making them feel guilty, your job is to help those children realize that the divorce was not their fault.

It will not be easy. Remember, their world has already been torn apart.

Gail

"Please don't blame the kids. I have been hurt by my stepson so many times I can't even count. I've felt so angry with him and have even sometimes felt the same way about him as I do about his mother. What I have come to understand is that, no matter how old he is (it seems like older children should know what they are doing), he is caught in a very painful situation. He has a very strong alliance with his mother and is very protective of her, even if it means lying for her. Even though he loves his father very much, I have to realize that he sees it as though his father left him, his mother didn't. He doesn't want to lose her too."

Lindsey

"I had three kids of my own when my two stepchildren came into my life. It's much easier to ease into parenthood than to have it dropped into your lap. You learn a few tricks of the trade along the way. I found that treating my stepchildren with the same love and tenderness as my own children was not the right thing to do. I was not their mother. They were used to a different kind of interaction with their biological mother.

"My suggestion to other women who might find themselves in this position is to try a different kind of adult role model, such as that of a teacher. Sometimes this is less threatening to them and easier for you as well. Try to relax and appreciate whatever joy the kids do provide. Let the small stuff slide, since the kids aren't around that much anyway."

Emphasize for the kids the value of their new extended family. Instead of losing a family, they now have even more people in their lives to love and care for them. They have more aunts, uncles, cousins, and grandparents with whom they can talk, play, and discuss their problems. It may be a unique perspective, but your stepkids must learn early on that life is only what we make it. We can choose to be happy and satisfied, in spite of all the bullshit we encounter, or we can let it all get to us and be miserable. It's a choice we all have, regardless of our circumstances.

Most importantly, remember, they're just kids. Kids don't have the experience, neither do they have the perspective, to look at problems or life in the same way as adults. They never will have the opportunity to gain this experience or perspective unless someone in their lives takes the time to teach them. With your help and guidance, along with that of your husband, they have an excellent chance of growing up to be well-adjusted adults.

Debbie

"We've made it clear to all of the kids and all of the extended family that our most important relationship is with each other. Not that we don't love our children. We do. But we refuse to let the children or the ex-spouses dictate to us. We get frustrated sometimes, but we stand firmly together. We value our marriage and our love above everything else."

6

~The Dilemma of Divorced Fathers~

*D*ivorced fathers lose custody of their children in 95 percent of all divorce cases. The reason for this is based on biological reality. Mothers give birth; mothers nurse their young. Men are not mothers. Babies are totally dependent upon their mothers. "Motherhood is a biological fact," said Margaret Mead, "fatherhood merely a social invention."

As civilization progressed, this biological fact was incorporated into the society's perceived expectation of women. For many centuries, before the women's liberation movement ever existed, women were expected to marry, to bear children, and to be caretakers of their husbands and children. Women were considered property, owned by men, and subjected to the whims and laws of men. Women were not allowed to own property or real estate. Neither were they allowed to or expected to make decisions. There were a few notable exceptions, but for the most part, this was reality in the olden days.

Until the feminist movement began, women in the workplace were few and far between. Economic societies, dominated by men, did not allow women the freedom or privilege of earning an income for themselves. Thus, in those rare cases when divorce did occur, the mother was awarded custody and the father was expected to continue to support his former family with child support and alimony.

Although times have changed in regard to society's views and expectations of women, and in regard to the opportunities available to women, the courts still act as if all women are helpless and walking around barefoot and pregnant. Even though it is a fact that the job market has been open to women for more than thirty years (*For godsakes, why doesn't she get a job?*), an ex-wife can easily play the helpless "little woman" act in court and win a free ride for life, as if nothing has changed for fifty years.

Today, in spite of calls for equality, courts still award sole custody to the mother. Demands for equality are only considered worthy when the demand is made by women. Equality in custody cases? Forget it. Most fathers don't have a chance in court. Even if he has been a loving, attentive father, upon divorce he is reduced to nothing more than a mere visitor in his children's lives and a fountain of free cash.

Whereas in a biofamily both parents interact with their children on a daily basis, the divorced father is not permitted this basic parental privilege. Ex-wives complain night and day about not getting enough money, but they can't fathom the pain of losing their children, of having their children ripped out of their lives in a day.

Nobody understands the depth of this pain better than a divorced father. The divorced father misses his daily kisses, the tucking-in at bed time, the big sloppy hugs. Now a tangential part of his own children's lives, he is only allowed certain specific time periods during which he may even lay eyes on them. No more horsey rides in the backyard. No more helping on with the backpack or tousling of the golden curls during a spontaneous game of Checkers. Divorced fathers miss the day-to-day thrill of watching their children grow. No amount of visitation can compensate for what the father loses or, for that matter, what the child loses when the father is shut out of the child's life.

John

"When I was still married, I could go into my son's room at night, *without permission,* and kiss him goodnight or pull the covers up over him. If I had a spare hour or so, we could go out into the backyard and play catch. If I was doing some chores around the house, I could show him how to use a screwdriver or a hammer, and explain what I was doing. I didn't have to ask my wife's permission. Suddenly, I need to make an appointment with my former wife just to see or talk to my own son. I feel like an outsider, looking in through the window somehow."

Mary

"I'm so much in love with the most wonderful man, I can't believe that his ex-wife didn't appreciate what she had. I realize that he never intends to remarry. He was burned so bad by the miserable witch. His view of marriage is that it is nothing more than a contract which requires a man to be financially responsible for a woman for the rest of her life, whether they are married or not. I'm scared. I'd always dreamed of being married and having a family of my own. I know this will never happen. I realize that I have a decision to make. Is the love I feel worth losing those things I'd always dreamed of?"

Karla

"I understand how difficult and painful divorce can be. But what I don't understand is the many members of my own sex who can be so vindictive and cruel. Not only do they *not* do what is right, they don't even think about the best interests of the children. Unfortunately, many seem to get away with murder. I am growing disgusted with the members of my sex selling all women out to be nothing more than helpless victims. I have never felt so much rage or disgust with my own sex as I have felt in my fiancé's divorce case."

A divorced father may be so spent that he is unable to afford another relationship, financially or emotionally. Since the ex-wife was probably awarded the house and everything in it, his first priority is to find another place to live. Then he has to buy a lot of the basic necessities for his new "bachelor pad," such as dishes, glasses, pots and pans, furniture, linens, etc., because all those things stayed with the house that his ex-wife kept. More than likely, he probably rented a furnished studio apartment and was lucky to afford the deposit to get the electricity turned on. Then the guy has to figure out how to support himself on approximately half a paycheck because, according to the law, spousal support and child support come first. A divorced father is fortunate if he can afford to keep a roof over his head, much less buy groceries.

Most states have certain child support formulas that they claim to follow. Depending upon the state, either the gross income or the net income of the biological parents is calculated and then combined. According to this combined income, a certain monetary figure is derived from the table to determine the amount of money required to support a child based upon the child's age. The figure obtained from this table is usually for one child and, therefore, doubled or tripled if necessary for two or more children.

Recently, some states have come up with the stupid idea of revoking the licenses of divorced fathers who are behind in their child support obligations. Score one more for an incongruous legal system. These new statutes include revoking everything from driver's licenses to business licenses to fishing licenses. Think about this for just a minute or two. If the man is already behind in making his payments, how in the hell is revoking his driver's license or business license going to make him pay? If he cannot drive to work or conduct business, exactly where is he supposed to get the money to pay his child support? And what's the point of revoking someone's fishing license? It might be a divorced father's only chance to get himself a decent meal!

It's not as if the divorced father hasn't been punished enough. He's already lost at least half of his income. He can no longer walk through the door of the house he worked so hard to buy. His kids have been torn out of his life. Maybe he loses his job and he falls behind on child support, so let's take away his driver's license. Now he can't even look for a job, because if he's caught driving with a revoked license, his ass is going to be sitting in jail.

Now who's going to provide for the children? Where's the logic? Where is the rational justification for this ridiculous policy? Who will put the brakes on the political judges and angry administrators who often demand that the father pay twice what he is able to pay?

Maria

"My husband wasn't even married to the bitch. She didn't even inform him that he was a father until two years after the birth. We were married in the interim. Ever since the paternity suit and the resulting child support obligation, she now takes home more money that he does, *tax free*. If I wasn't working, we would be unable to pay the rent."

Maria is not the only second wife supporting her husband and family on her own salary.

June

"My husband's ex-wife has an attitude that my husband has no rights whatsoever to any information about his daughter because *she* has custody. I can't understand how your rights to have access to your child can be determined by how much money you might have to fight for them."

Diane

"It breaks my heart to realize the pain my husband goes through every day. I'm angry with the system. It's so fucked up. All he's done is move across the country, pay every damn penny of support on time, put up with her crap, drive extra miles unnecessarily only to be shut down by a legal system that condones irresponsible behavior by a woman who isn't fit to be a mother."

Elaine

"My husband's ex-wife lives in the former marital home rent free, due to the fact that she also owns two rentals that pay her approximately $800 per month. The money from these rentals pays her mortgage payment. She also collects child support. Of course, along with the house, she kept the big-screen TV, the computer, all the furniture, all the appliances, as well as the family car. Does she sound destitute to you? We just found out today that not only is she somehow managing to get food stamps, she is also collecting AFDC, and on Medicaid as well. Can you believe it? And we're barely keeping a roof over our heads!"

In an article in *The Christian Science Monitor* (June 22, 1990), a study was reported by Fathers for Equality and Justice in Wisconsin. According to this study, in which 252 cases were examined, only 22 fathers (nine percent) were able to maintain a primary role in their children's lives. The other 230 fathers settled for subordinate positions regarding the care and custody of their children.

Cynics are quick to assert that men simply don't care. The evidence, however, indicates that men surrender without a fight because they feel that the system is against them. Family law professionals themselves admit that being a good father isn't enough to gain custody. The mother must be proved unfit, somehow, which is a difficult task to accomplish. In an newspaper article in the *Sierra Vista Herald* (January 21, 1997), one attorney, himself a divorced father, said, "In order for a father to get custody in this country, the wife has to be physically abusive, a drug addict, or a prostitute who has just murdered the mayor of a major city."

Tina

"For every divorced mother who enjoys custody of her children, there is a father who misses those same children. We rarely hear about the heartache and pain that a father feels when the mother chooses to divorce him and force him out of the daily lives of his children."

Moreover, there is a tendency for the noncustodial parent (your husband) to become over-indulgent and lenient when it comes to disciplining his children, a symptom of what I cynically refer to as the 'limp dick syndrome.' Let's face it. He's been hurt. He's lost his children once already. He's afraid that if he disciplines them in any way that he'll alienate them even further and they won't come to visit. His ex-wife is no help whatsoever because her sole motivation is to turn the kids against him, no matter what the cost—to him or the kids. So, he lets them have their way.

These feelings are understandable. However, the hesitancy to discipline due to these feelings is not good for the kids. Their lives are already in turmoil. What they need most is discipline and structure. Your husband's fear of losing his children again can create real problems for your marriage. A husband who doesn't back you up in the area of discipline, whether the kids involved are yours or his, is no better than a limp dick. He's there but he does nothing for you. With recovery, however, will come strength.

Fran

"The worst mistake a second wife can make is thinking that she won't resent or be jealous of his ex-wife. I simmered every time she called, usually on the pretense of needing to talk about the kids. It went on forever. My husband is a calm, easy-going type of person, and I'm still angry at him for not standing up to her and for allowing her to do anything and everything she wanted. She even had the nerve to tell me in the beginning that she didn't want him anymore, but she didn't want anyone else to have him, either."

Kids are intelligent little creatures and fast learners. They feel secure when parents set limits for them and they need to know that there are going to be consequences for their behavior, good or bad. Kids are also flexible. They can and will adapt.

They will, however, test you to see what and how much they can get away with, especially if there are no rules at their mom's house. They perceive their father's weakness and they might try to manipulate it to their own advantage or play one household against the other.

Adam

"I grew up in a divorced home, and whenever my mom wouldn't buy me something I wanted, I'd call my dad. He usually came through for me. I just used it as a way to get whatever I wanted. Whenever I didn't like what my stepmother said, I would say something like, 'I don't have to do what you say because you aren't my mom.' I know it hurt her but at the time I didn't care."

The ex-wife-from-hell, the one who never got her *real* divorce, actually finds pleasure in the strife she causes between your husband and his children. She is utterly unconcerned about the impact on the children's lives. All she cares about is using the kids to maintain some kind of demented control over your husband.

Concerned, loving mothers don't play head games with their children. Concerned, loving mothers don't try to force their children to choose between their mother and their father, regardless of the circumstances surrounding the divorce.

Whatever you do, don't let her cause fights or come in between you and your husband. Don't let her use your husband's children to tear your marriage apart.

Fran

"My husband provides full transportation (an eight-hour round trip) while she dictates the times, dates, etc. I don't understand why, but she decided we should have my husband's daughter from the day after Christmas through December 30th. Then our stepdaughter calls, the day before school gets out, and tells us that her mother wants us to pick her up on the 21st and return her back to her mother by

1:00 p.m. on Christmas Day. I just get so angry that our plans and lives are constantly revolving around what his ex-wife wants."

Gail

"My husband lets his ex-wife dictate to him whatever visitation she sees fit, and believe you me, she doesn't manage to see much, regardless of what the court orders say. He just lets her do it, and it makes me so mad. She changes plans at the last minute, sometimes he's already been on his way to pick the kids up when she calls. I have no way of getting in touch with him. Then when he gets there and she doesn't show up with the kids, he has another two-hour ride to get back home. I could just scream!"

If your husband's ex-wife-from-hell is interfering with court-ordered visitation, there are several possible ways to handle this. The first would be to encourage your husband to sit down with his ex-wife and discuss the problem in a calm and rational manner. Sure, and if there was some sort of magic formula to make that happen, you'd sell it to the highest bidder. I only threw that one in for the fun of it.

The second is a more practical approach. Your husband should keep a copy of the divorce decree in the car, just in case he goes to pick the kids up and, for whatever reason, the ex-wife simply won't let the kids leave. He can then go to the nearest police station and file a complaint against her for interference with a court order.

It's a fairly simple procedure with no cost to the complaining party, which is the best part for you and your husband. A police officer listens to your story, reads the decree and, maybe after a phone call to the ex-wife advising her to follow the court order, files charges with the County Attorney. When the case is prosecuted, your husband will be required to go to court as a witness. Her offense is a Class 1 misdemeanor in some states and can result in a fine of up to $2,500. Make sure to keep a log of all the days and times visitation was denied or interfered with in some way. This will help your case when you get to court.

The third method would be to save every penny you can, hire a lawyer, and go back to court to modify the divorce decree. You and your husband together might even file for custody, if circumstances warrant this. This method can be expensive, however, as you probably already know. However, if the ex-wife-from-hell happens to accumulate any charges for interference with a court order, this would benefit your husband's custody case, and you could have her charged with contempt as well. You might not actually win custody, but each and every chink in the armor helps all fathers gain rights, and it will give you a lift to be the one dragging *her* into court for once.

As a second wife, you have to decide how much of yourself you want to invest in this fight, not just financially but emotionally as well. Maybe you've seen that look on his face after a long ride home from a visit that didn't happen and you've had enough. Maybe you damn well know the kids would be better off with their father and you than they are with their mother. Or maybe you've had all the fight fought out of you already and you just want to let it all go.

Sometimes it feels as if the strain will take you down. Sometimes the tension in your marriage seems like a tight rope that you don't want to walk anymore. But, day by day, you will hang on. You will fight for your husband and for yourself because, even from behind the eight ball, you can see the true picture. Millions of women feel the way you feel. Millions of children are missing out on the fathers who are as loving and responsible as the man you married. You will not give up. You cannot give up.

Remember, he loves you. He does not love her anymore. You might not "feel his pain," but you sure see it day by day. And you feel the burden of supporting a family all by yourself, while his ex-wife whines about her tax-free income. You see these things and you feel them and you are not alone. You work like a dog, you give up so much, you struggle to care for children not your own and you are not alone. You are a second wife, the better choice. She was and is still is the big mistake in your husband's life. There are many like her, wailing all the time. But there are many like you, second wives engaged in the silent struggle.

But what good does that do, you may ask. What good can it do? We are all aware that our court system is strongly biased in favor of the mother and against the father. Your husband lost custody of the children and all he can do is *visit* his own kids. This is perhaps the most tragic element of divorce in this nation.

Any yet, even those visits are often withheld. Every day of the week, in each and every state, custodial mothers deny visitation to fathers. It happens all the time. They get away with it because they're in total control of the situation. The courts will always side with what the first wife says, regardless of the facts.

In fact, some believe that the activists in the legal system would like to do away with visitation all together. They certainly refuse to connect it to child support. And yet, does it not follow that if your husband is doing his part, his ex-wife should do hers? Unfortunately, there is never any connection between the two in the eyes of the law. One can't help but suspect that the divorce and family courts and, indeed, society view fathers as utterly expendable, except when it's time to pay the bills.

Deborah

"There are times when I would just love to grab the bitch by the neck and shake the crap out of her. She controls everything in regards to my stepson. She makes all the decisions. The courts are on her side no matter what we say."

Arlene

"My husband's ex denies visitation, refuses to let my husband even talk to the kids on the telephone, lies to the kids about us, changes visitation at the drop of a hat, and tells the kids they don't have to listen to me. The list goes on and on. I'm beginning to think that there is no limit as to how low she will go. We're running out of money to fight her in court because the judge believes whatever she says, even when we've had evidence to prove she was lying!"

As we all know, if the father misses just one child support payment, he's likely to face charges of contempt. He might land in jail. His wages will be garnished. Just imagine if the whole scenario were turned around and your husband could pay or not whenever he felt like it, but his ex-wife would be thrown in jail for thwarting even one visit. It sounds so ridiculous, but the opposite is common place. So much for equality.

Many second wives feel frustrated with the system. It's easy to get cynical. But the way you deal with this frustration will have a tremendous impact on your life and on your marriage. Will you be strong enough to cope with the injustice and yet, somehow, manage to keep your marriage intact? Remember, you're not the only second wife feeling this way or searching for answers. Although our circumstances are unique, there are certainly enough similarities in every second marriage to learn from the experience of others. Sometimes, just knowing that others are experiencing similar ordeals gives us strength.

Ultimately, we will have to join together to fight for the real meaning of equality and that won't be easy. It's a knee-jerk response to feminist demands to give women custody every time but, as we have learned the hard way, it is not always best for the children and it's certainly not the exercise of "equal rights."

7

~Deadbeat Moms~

*E*veryone knows about Deadbeat Dads. They are constantly in the news, the subject of legislation, the butt of bad jokes, the topic of talk shows, the cause of all that's wrong with America. Yeah, yeah, we know about them. But this country has a dirty little secret that is never talked about, don't we? Yes, we do. Deadbeat Moms.

The deadbeat mom can be defined as a mother who abandons her children emotionally and physically after a divorce, sometimes even earlier. Of course, she abandons them financially, as well. The deadbeat mom does not want the responsibility of being a parent. She has no desire to be bothered with runny noses, potty training, sticky hands, or questions. She wants her freedom and her independence. The deadbeat mom wants to be able to go out and party at the drop of a hat, to do whatever she wants whenever she wants. Kids tie you down. Kids need love and stability. Kids need adults who will take the time to teach them and to answer their questions. Kids can be a real pain in the ass, let's face it. The deadbeat mom simply does not want them.

For now.

If you're a second wife who happens to be married to the rare divorced father who has custody of his children, perhaps you thought that you and your husband and the children would be living without interference from your husband's ex-wife. After all, she took off. She proclaimed her disinterest in her own children. She abandoned them. She gave up her rights, didn't she?

No way. One thing about the deadbeat mom: she tends to come back. A unique type of ex-wife-from-hell, here is a divorced mother who was perfectly happy to abdicate her responsibility *until you came along.* She has had minimal contact with her children since she bailed out. She might have shown up once in a blue moon, or not. Every so often, if the kids were lucky, she'd send a Christmas present or a birthday card. Every once in a while, she'd call them. She made it obvious that she wasn't in it for the long haul. She had her own agenda, and she never allowed her own children to interfere with her life-style.

Your husband has told you all about her. He is the one who held it all together when Mommy decided to take off. One of the things that attracted you to your husband was the fact that he was an excellent father. You were willing to be a surrogate mother, to assist him in the raising of his children, to step in where their own mother wasn't willing, to nurture these sad kids and to be there for them. Eventually, you thought, you and your husband could have a child together and create a big happy family.

This is the kind of thing that can really piss off a deadbeat mom. It's not that she cares one fucking bit about the kids' welfare. She's already proven that she couldn't care less about what happens to them. The only thing that she does care about is the fact that you, her kids, and her ex-husband are a family.

Suddenly, the deadbeat mom takes an interest. Why? Because you have something she doesn't have. A loving husband, perhaps. You're happy; she's not. Your husband has managed to go on with his life, something she never thought he would be able to do. She assumed that he

84

would mope around for the rest of his life, struggling to take care of the kids, and missing her, begging her to come back. The kids were supposed to be depressed because they idolized her and missed her. They were not supposed to find solace in a loving, better woman who is not their natural mother, but who loves them nevertheless.

Nobody was supposed to go on. Everyone was supposed to wait for Ms. Deadbeat Mom to come back. Then you came along. You, the enemy. He married again and you have made her broken family whole again . . . without her. What's a miserable selfish bitch to do? She does the only thing that can really hurt you now—she shows up out of the clear blue sky and starts interfering with your life.

The phone rings.

"Hello."

"Hello. May I speak to John?"

"May I tell him who's calling, please?"

"No, you may not. Just let me speak to him."

"John, there's some woman on the phone and she won't tell me who she is."

Deep down, of course, you know it's *her.* You hand your husband the phone. You can tell by the look on his face that you were right. It's his ex-wife, the good-for-nothing bitch-from-hell. You walk around the corner and eavesdrop, or maybe you just stand right there and listen.

In the short conversation your husband doesn't say much. Then he hangs up and says:

"Annette wants to see the kids. She's going to pick them up tomorrow for a couple of days."

"Just like that? Where has she been for the last four years?"

"I don't know. What can I say? Maybe she's had a change of heart. She is their mother, after all."

"And what am I? Chopped liver? Who has been taking care of them for the last four years? Who has been getting up at night when they're sick? Who makes sure they get to soccer practice on time? Who makes sure they have clean clothes and food to eat? Did you even bother to ask her where the hell she's been or what the hell she's been doing?"

"I'm sorry. What was I supposed to say?"

These conversations are going to happen and they might make you begin to wonder if your husband is married to her or to you. However, you know that your husband is just an all-around nice guy. If he wasn't, he'd tell the bitch to go screw herself. But he does understand the basic, instinctive, biological love that his children have for their mother, even if she is a worthless piece of shit. He knows that she has caused his kids pain and, if he can, he wants to help ease that pain. Even if his ex-wife doesn't deserve the time of day, he is willing, for the sake of the kids, to let her assume her role as mother in his children's lives.

It's not that he doesn't appreciate everything you've done over the years, or that he is trying to demean the role that you play in his children's lives. Far from it. This situation is comparable to that of adopted children who grow up and want to search for their biological parents. The adopted children still love and appreciate everything that their adoptive parents have done for them. Somehow, though, there is an inborn compulsion that draws them toward their biological parents.

What can you do? What the hell can you do? No matter what, you're going to be wrong. The outsider. The intruder. If you say something to your husband, he gets defensive. If you don't say anything, you hate yourself. The kids, of course, are thrilled to see her. You can understand; and yet, you don't understand. After all, you're the one who has been there for them. You're the only *real* mother they know. Why should they be so happy to see this worthless woman, this piece of trash, who doesn't give a rat's ass about her own kids' welfare? It doesn't make sense.

She's baaaaaack! The deadbeat mom is now your problem; she's calling your husband, coming over, taking the kids away. You have to decide how far you're going to let her go because she will go just as far as you let her. Make no mistake about it, her goal is to disrupt and ruin your family's happiness. This is entirely common sense, even though it may be obvious only to you. If she didn't care about her children before she found out about you, the only reason she's interfering now is because she's jealous of your relationship with her children and of your relationship with her ex-husband. She never got her *real* divorce.

Crystal

"Kids love both their parents. They have a right to do so and anything other than support for that love is essentially degrading the child. Although it's been painful for all of us, the situation finally came to a point where not discussing things with the kids would be worse for them than knowing some of the truth. One night, I found my stepdaughter crying in bed. *'Why did Mom leave me to go to Texas?'* How do you answer a question like that? The only answer I could come up with was that maybe her mom needed some time to work out her own problems and just wasn't in a position to handle the family."

Marla

"I never could understand how a mother could give up a two-year-old child. Even though she had custody, she basically dumped the kid on my husband's doorstep and nobody saw or heard from her for eight years. All of a sudden, out of the clear-blue sky, she shows up, wanting to resume her position as mother. She even took us to court! Thankfully, the judge didn't go for it, although he did allow her to have limited visitation. Her guilt trips have begun to take a toll on our son, though. He's beginning to believe her lies and I'm scared for him. She left him one time and she might do it again."

There's something about being abandoned by one's mother that haunts a person for life.

Jimmy

"I cried myself to sleep so many nights, I can't even begin to count. What did I ever do that made my mother leave and never come back? It wasn't until I was older that I understood that it wasn't me, it was her. But even the realization of the truth never did make the pain go away."

Jon

"We wouldn't see our mother for years at a time. All of a sudden, she'd just show up. Don't ask me why. I can't explain it to this day, but we would be so happy to see her! She'd buy us a few toys, sometimes something big like a new bike, then she'd be gone again. We would cry for a few days, then life just went on. My stepmother was the one who was always there for us. She bandaged our knees when we fell down; she sat up with us when we were little and when we were too sick to sleep; she held us in her arms and comforted us. It wasn't until a few years ago that I told my stepmother how much I appreciated everything she had done for us. I know we hurt her over the years, but she stuck it out. She is our real mother."

The deadbeat mom is very, very skillful at avoiding responsibility. She's equally as adept in manipulating her children's natural love for her against their father and against you. You have an ordeal in your life that is never talked about, as if the deadbeat mom does not even exist. But some of us know otherwise, don't we? We've seen the children's tears, our husband's predicament as he tries to help them, and the awful, degrading position she has carved out for you, the stepmother.

The deadbeat mom leaves behind her a heartless trail of anger, hurt, and tears. As soon as it seems to settle, she returns to stir it all up again. And so on, and so on. The hurt will never go away, not for you, your husband, or the children. But, thankfully, all children do grow up, become adults, and eventually they come to realize and reckon with the truth. So hang in there, because when that day comes, they will be thanking you and loving you . . . not her.

8
~Blended Families~

Remember all those wonderful fairy tales you heard as a kid? You know—the theme is always the same—Prince Charming rescues the Beautiful Princess (from the wicked stepmother), kisses her, and they fall in love forever. Happy endings are hard to resist. Perhaps you imagined that the man of your dreams would come along and carry you off to a castle somewhere. Of course, you'd have two lovely little children and live happily ever after.

Fairy tales are awfully comforting, but the onset of adulthood usually dispels most of the more fabulous elements lodged in our collective subconscious. One day you wake up and find that life isn't anything like a fairy tale. Still, we can't help but hope sometimes. We'd like fabulous vacations, million-dollar homes, and designer wardrobes. But how many of us will ever afford those things? Reality sets in.

First, though, let's take a look at how our reality is shaped by conventional wisdom and assumptions. What do people assume when they hear the term, "second wife"? Well, the modern-day stereotype has you married to a very wealthy middle-aged business man who callously dumped his noble and flawless first wife in exchange for you. And who are you? Why you're a very young, big-busted, tiny-wasted, blond bimbo who used her seething, unbridled sexuality to lure the hapless (yet despicable) rich family man away from his perfect wife. See yourself here in this picture? You home-wrecker! You slut!

Propaganda is not your friend. These stereotypes let people go around thinking the worst of you and the best of themselves. It lets them off the hook. No one sympathizes with real second wives, everyday women who work night and day and endure hardships most women can't imagine for the sake of a loving marriage and a happy home.

No, you won't get any sympathy from daytime television or the movie of the week. But you will get solace and hope for a happy future by shutting all of that out and giving yourself credit for who and what you are. You love this man, in spite of all the trouble and baggage. You want a life with him. It's also natural to want to have a baby with the man you love.

Contrary to the laughable image of the trophy wife living in luxury, however, your child's quality of life is going to be deeply affected by hardships that never touch most children. If you already have a child (or children) and if your husband is trying to deal with an ex-wife-from-hell, paying an ungodly amount of child support and coping with lawyers, then you understand what it's all about. If you're still in the dreaming stage and you're thinking, *"baby of our own, baby of our own,"* then your collision with reality lies ahead.

Let's say that your husband is already paying child support for one or more children from a former marriage. Often a full 30 to 40 percent of his income is already out the door. This percentage varies and, in some instances, can be as high as 80 percent. It depends upon your state, the number of children, the hostility of the judge, and the ex-wife's degree of greed.

Most states now take the second wife's income into consideration in figuring the amount of child support due to the first wife. In other words, you and your husband can end up paying either his whole income or even an amount in excess of his whole income to his ex-wife. Let's see, if they're taking more than he makes, where is that extra money coming from? From you! That's who. And those are the sweetest dollars for her—the ones that come right out of your paycheck. Talk about getting screwed.

Furthermore, the divorce and family courts do not view all children equally. In the eyes of the law, children born of a first marriage have more economic value than those born of a second marriage. The first children are worthy of support. The children of a second marriage are viewed as second-class citizens. Her children are simply worth more to society than your children. Lawyers will be the first to tell you this.

Mary

"While contesting a request for an increase in child support by my husband's ex-wife, we were told by our lawyer that the fact that my husband has other children to support is irrelevant. The judge couldn't care less. The viewpoint of the court, as well as that of society in general, is that divorced fathers shouldn't have any more children if they are having difficulty providing for children from a previous marriage. I was told that if I wanted the court to take my child into consideration, that I should divorce my husband. Only then would the court consider my child to have any value whatsoever, which is the amount of child support that my husband would be obligated to pay."

Of course, an ex-wife is free to remarry and have as many children as she wants without any legal impact on her child support payments whatsoever. Even if she marries a millionaire, your husband still has to pay her as before. And yet, if a father remarries, his new wife and children are beneath the fair consideration of the court.

Lori

"When my husband's ex-wife found out about my new baby she tried to get the court to "terminate" his paternity rights. The female judge screamed and yelled at my husband in open court, declaring, 'This child does not exist!' But he does exist, very much, bless his heart. When he was about four years old, and still a Disney fan, he gave my husband's ex-wife a nickname: *Cruella*. Of course, it stuck."

Barbara

"The lawyer said, 'You should have known what you were getting into when you married him. His kids from the first marriage were born first and are more important than yours.' "

Kara

"The judge asked my husband, 'Why did you have more kids when you can't even support the ones you have already?'"

This is really the crux of the issue, the heart of this book. Judges reflect a society, and this society is saying that you and your children have no right to exist. If you questioned 100 people on the street, they would probably agree. They would ask if your husband's first wife was completely satisfied with her support (as if any ex-wife ever is) and they would say that you and your children have no right to exist if the answer to that question is no.

Rarely does a society turn its back on such a large group of women and children. Fortunately for us, they don't throw stones, but often second wives feel as if that is what they are doing, especially in court. It is a strong, visceral, and powerful attitude that pervades our society and every second wife must reckon with it if she is to be honest with herself. No one tells the children of welfare-dependent adolescent mothers that they should not exist. No judge ever tells the offspring of criminals that they don't exist. Only second wives and their children are subjected to this hideous social policy. Only women and children who function productively within loving families are told that they have no right to exist.

With our 50 percent divorce rate, isn't it time to recognize that children born of a second marriage are as valuable as children of a first marriage? Perhaps if child support guidelines were at all fair, and *both* parents were considered responsible for the support of a child, then fathers wouldn't bear the whole burden for two sets of kids.

No one shouts, whines, and complains on national television when second wives work overtime and bear the whole burden of support for their families. Yet, millions of first wives refuse to go to work. They act like children who must be supported for life. Old, helpless, greedy children. But first wives are not children, they are adults. Each of them should be working to provide half the support for their children. Why is society so threatened by this simple concept of shared responsibility?

Of course, it is the children who suffer from these hateful social attitudes. They didn't chose to be born in a first or a second marriage. One child has the protection of law, the courts, the state, and another child is left with nothing. The system is corrupt and biased because the society is that way. Even though divorce is legal, and even though 75 percent of all divorces are filed by women, men are punished for getting divorced. By extension, the man's new wife and children are punished as well. All for doing something that is entirely legal and sanctioned by society.

After a divorce, the first wife is allowed to have the life of her choice. She can remarry. She can have more children, if she wants to, and not lose any of the income from her first husband. The husband, however, is not allowed to live a life until the kids (whom he rarely even gets to see) reach the ripe old age of eighteen.

There is no limit to the number of times the ex-wife can keep coming back to the well. If he gets a raise, she can drag him back into court and force him to pay her even more. There is little incentive for the divorced man to work harder, to make more money, to try and improve his lot in life. Why should he? There is no benefit, not with an ex-wife sitting on her ass or hovering around with her lawyers, waiting for more money to come in just so she can scarf it up. No wonder guys go off the grid!

Recently, a few states have come up with something called Income Sharing Plans, designed so that a divorced father can afford to remarry and even have another child or two. Gee, thanks! The plan allows a credit for subsequent children born after the divorce in figuring the amount of child support to be paid to a first wife. The State of Washington, for example, uses what it calls the Whole Family Approach. All of the children, regardless of whether they're the result of a first or second marriage, are taken into consideration in the calculation of the child support payments. However, if the second wife has a substantial income, the father's child support payment to his ex-wife might be adjusted. Their logic is that if the second wife's income can be used to provide for their family's necessities, more of the father's income can be used to provide for children of his first marriage. If the ex-wife remarries and her husband's income is more than ample to provide for everyone in that family, then the father's support obligation might be reduced, especially if he is the sole support of his new family.

Well, it's a tiny step in the right direction. But if the new husband adopts the children (and this sometimes happens against the natural father's will), then the new husband should assume all support obligations, don't you think? Also, if the second wife works and the ex-wife doesn't (or refuses to), then the second wife's income should be off limits, don't you think?

Let's get back to the question of your new baby. Sometimes a divorced father is leery of going through the whole thing all over again, especially after being burned so badly the last time.

Tammy

"I want desperately to have a child of my own, but my husband is afraid of the effect it will have on his children. I think that there's more to it, but he's just using the kids as an excuse."

You love him and he loves you, but don't forget that he had children with another woman who is now his ex-wife. This same woman, whom he once loved and who supposedly once loved him, has now metamorphosed into a miserable, half-crazed, vindictive ex-wife-from-hell. How can he be sure this won't happen to him again? Put yourself in his shoes and try to understand how he feels.

Tara

"My husband and I have one child together. He's always known that I wanted her to have a brother or sister, but he told me that he didn't want any more kids, that he would be unable to handle it either mentally or physically."

Not all men feel this way, but you'll want to know in advance how your husband feels about having more children. If you do decide to have children, the courts and the lawyers will be against you. Another child might turn out to be a serious financial strain. On the other hand, will there ever really be enough money to go around? Why should she get to have babies and not you? You want all of your husband's fatherly love going only to her children? You know you'll be a better mother.

So, go for it. I'm not trying to discourage you from having children and raising a family with the man you love. No amount of money or convenience can compensate for the joy of having your own baby. I just want you to be realistic and be prepared. Don't think it will be easy or pleasant to be told that your baby is worth less than her baby.

Also consider factors other than money that might arise upon the joyous birth of your love child. Your husband's ex-wife, angry and bitter already, might explode with rage because you had a baby with her husband from whom she never got her *real* divorce. If she was trouble before, you ain't seen nothing yet. She and her lawyers can demand that everything you buy, every bill you pay, every step your take for the benefit of this baby, be justified against the needs of the "poor starving children" of your husband's first marriage. No matter how much he pays or what he does for them, it will not be enough in the eyes of the court if you have a baby of your own. Be prepared for this sick twist in the legal road. And remember, she might get even worse just at the time when you most need a break from her.

Later on, others will be affected by the new baby's presence. Your stepkids might envy the attention that their father gives to the new baby. They might feel as if they've been displaced somehow, that they're no longer loved, and respond to the new baby with varying degrees of rage or disinterest.

Try to be patient with them. Now your stepchildren find themselves involved in complex relationships that might still seem temporary to them. Their parents' marriage didn't last; they're not sure that yours will. Suddenly, they have stepbrothers and stepsisters in their lives. Suddenly, they're sharing their own father with the child of woman who is not their mother, and who knows how long all of this will last? Every other weekend, big stepbrother comes over and sees new little stepsister and he says to himself, why bother? Or a hoard of stepchildren (three seems like a hoard) descends upon your home every other Sunday and your baby cries from the tension of the crowd in the house. Your husband's children see the new baby, and who can really predict or know what they feel about it?

Jane

"How do you foster a sibling relationship when the time they spend together is sporadic at best? Should you feel guilty if you put your own child first, at least in your mind if not in practice? And, God forbid, what if something should happen to your husband? Your children may not have any contact at all with their (half/step) siblings until they are adults. How do you feel about the fact that you may have to sacrifice giving things to your own child because the money has to go to child support, alimony, and attorneys?"

Competition. Resentment. Jealousy. Anger. Fear. Go ahead, have a baby! Just like everything else in the life of a second wife, it's very complicated. Of course, if you hated complications, you wouldn't have married him in the first place, would you? If you were too weak to handle it, you would have turned your back on the man you love and waited around for Joe Single to come along and make you a first wife. In other words, you wouldn't be you.

In spite of all the troubles, the propaganda, the legal problems, believe it or not, second families are usually happier. They're the result of two mature people choosing each other, correcting the bad mistakes in the first marriage, and embarking on the challenges of parenthood with their eyes wide open.

Tina

"The last few years have had their ups and downs, but I wouldn't trade them for the world. What makes it work is sticking together through thick or thin. My husband loves me and I love him. I can't help it if his ex was too stupid to realize what she had. I treasure what I have. Our baby is everybody's baby, a wonderful bond joining all of us together."

Marilee

"I was fearful of what the reaction of my stepkids would be when they found out I was pregnant. I worried for nothing. They were excited at the prospect of having a baby in the house. They've been so much help. The only problem we really had was the kids arguing as to whose turn it was to hold or bathe the baby!"

Jamie

"Instead of worrying about what we can't buy for our baby, we focus on the importance of what a healthy relationship can offer to her."

Donna

"There was a span of ten years between the kids from my first marriage and the two from my second marriage. But the second time around was so much easier. For one thing, my husband helped out, something my ex never did. And the kids were terrific. They were old enough to really be of help, not just in the way. They entertained the little ones and kept them busy while my husband and I prepared dinner. After dinner, they were old enough to clean up the kitchen while we bathed the babies. It worked out great. I thought I was crazy myself to even attempt to have a second family but I don't regret one minute."

If your financial situation is tight, your children might end up wearing hand-me-downs all their lives. So what? Millions of kids have worn hand-me-downs without any problem. You'll find that they really don't mind. And if find yourself turning to friends and family for help now and then, well, isn't that what they're for? Helping one another is what it's all about. It strengthens our bonds and builds a strong extended family, which is worth much more than anything money can buy.

Children born in second families thrive on the love in their homes. They absorb the joy and appreciation their parents feel from just having found each other and from being together. The truth is that your baby is a love child. It might sound 1960's corny, but love at conception does matter. Whatever society says, whatever the legal system says, the fact that your baby was wanted, dreamed of, planned, and sacrificed for makes him or her a very special child. But you already know that, don't you.

9
~*Fathers' Rights*~

*A*ll indications are clear that children living in a single-parent home suffer in ways that children raised by two loving parents do not. The studies have been done. The research is in. Children need two parents. The importance of a father's role in the life of a child simply cannot be underestimated.

If a parent dies and a child grows up without one parent no one tries to downplay the significance of that experience or the pain that it causes to the child. Yes, the child survives it. Children can survive any number of horrible and painful experiences, but the fact that the loss of the parent could not be avoided affects the child's response to the loss.

However, when a child loses a father to divorce, when visitation is denied, when the father is excluded by the ex-wife and by the court from the day-to-day life of the child, there is no avoiding the blame for the pain caused to that child. The blame rests squarely on those who devalue fathers and cast them as merely sources of financial support rather than the full-fledged parents they can and want to be.

Children of divorce often have problems that are caused by this severing of relationships. In an article in the *American Journal of Orthopsychiatry* (October 1987), called "Long-Term Effects of Divorce on Children: A Developmental Vulnerability Model," Dr. Kalter observes that "Among teenage and adult populations of females, parental divorce has been associated with lower self-esteem, precocious sexual activity, greater delinquent-like behavior, and more difficulty in establishing gratifying, lasting, adult heterosexual relationships."

Of course, little girls suffer when they lose their daddies. No experience in life can replace the childhood experience of being daddy's little girl. A loving mother does not deny her daughter this experience. Take away a little girl's daddy, and she grows up mistrusting men, reacting with intensified anxiety to separation, living in denial, and perhaps avoiding all of the feelings associated with the loss.

Sons who lose their fathers suffer in a myriad of ways and experience equally harmful although different reactions to their fatherless childhood. Often angry and belligerent, boys who have been denied their fathers and have had their fathers' images poisoned can develop an underlying rage that can surface in unpredictable and destructive ways.

Both boys and girls who grow up without their fathers are inclined to have more difficulties in school. "In summary, 30 percent of the children in the present study experienced a marked decrease in academic performance following parental separation, and this was evident three years later," say Drs. Bisnaire, Firestone, and Rynard in their article, "Factors Associated with Academic Achievement in Children Following Parental Separation," *(American Journal of Orthopsychiatry*, January 1990).

Children growing up without their fathers have a tendency to drop out of school, have lower self-esteem, and are predisposed to delinquent behavior such as joining gangs. "Developmental and relationship theory should have alerted the mental health field to the potential immediate and long-range consequences for the child of only seeing a parent four days each month. And yet, until recently, there was no particular challenge to this traditional post-divorce parenting arrangement, despite growing evidence that such post-divorce relationships were not sufficiently nurturing or stabilizing for many children and parents," says Dr. Joan Kelly in *Joint Custody and Shared Parenting*, p. 85.

As far back as the 1980's, people began to notice a dangerous trend. "Nearly 80 percent of adolescents in psychiatric hospitals come from broken homes," noted *The Journal of the American Academy of Child and Adolescent Psychiatry*, in a 1988 article, "Parental Functioning and the Home Environment in Families of Divorce."

Boys from families with absent fathers are at a higher risk for violent behavior than boys from intact families. According to the U.S. Department of Health and Human Services' Survey on Child Health (1993), kids living in homes without a stepfather or without contact with their biological father are twice as likely to drop out of school. Seventy-two percent of adolescent murderers grew up without a father and 60 percent of America's rapists grew up without a father. Fatherless children are at a dramatically greater risk of suicide.

In 1990, the Bureau of Justice Statistics conducted an in-depth survey of prisoners in 45 states. According to this study, more than half of all inmates did not live with both parents while growing up. Think about this one fact for just a minute or two. The particular offense committed was not considered. The study sought to identify the circumstances in which the prisoners grew up. Half did not have two parents. Conceivably, a percentage of these prisoners wouldn't be in prison right now if there had been a caring, prevalent father-figure in their lives.

Despite the research and evidence which prove that fathers play an important role in their children's lives, the courts continue to award sole custody almost exclusively to mothers. Lawyers tell fathers not to bother to request custody. Judges order fathers out of their children's lives every day. Clever and destructive ways of cutting off a custody claim have been developed that cast a father as abusive or even as a sexual deviant, all with the goal of removing the father from the child's life, except financially of course. Did you know that an ex-wife can claim abuse *by fax* and get a restraining order *the very same day* that prevents the father from coming near his own children?

Even if a father is an active participant in his children's lives one day—feeding them breakfast, playing with them in the afternoon, reading them stories, and tucking them into bed, he can be easily shut out by an angry ex-wife. And who is to say what a good father really is? Does doing dishes make a man a good father? Or is that some feminist construct of the ideal helpmate? Does following politically correct proclamations deem this father worthy and that one unworthy? Funny how some of the most unconventional and "incorrect" fathers end up being loved and adored by their children. Who is to say?

In fact, it doesn't really matter whether he is a good father or not. If an ex-wife wants to sever his relationship with his children, her methods and avenues are numerous. Her sacred claim to sole custody is rarely questioned. After a divorce, a loving father is lucky even to see his kids for four lousy days out of the month.

In the book, *Divided Families* (1991), Cherlin and Furstenberg state that 40 percent of children living in fatherless homes haven't seen their fathers in one year or more. Only one in five of these children have had the opportunity to spend even one night a week at their father's home.

Even among fathers who regularly maintain contact with their children after divorce, the relationship between fathers and children changes dramatically. Instead of being a guiding figure, a constant presence, the father becomes a visitor. He and the children might go to the movies, out for a hamburger, or spend a couple of hours together playing ball on Saturday afternoon. Then he takes the kids home and that's all the interaction they have for another week or two. This is not real fatherhood. It is not the kind of solid presence one must have in the child's life in order to become a guiding influence. Only sharing time fifty/fifty with the mother can give the father an opportunity to raise and provide for his children properly.

In response to the unbearable injustice and pain of losing their children, some divorced fathers have joined together to fight the system. Suffering every day, missing their children, and longing for the chance to be part of their lives, they are working to change the status quo. Born out of a horrible necessity and in reaction to many bad laws, these groups try to help fathers find their way through the darkly biased hallways of divorce and family court.

Some of the groups are more radical than others. Some fathers groups advocate sole father custody. Some hearken back to the old days of the patriarchy. But most of them simply strive for fairness. Primarily, they seek to ensure their continuing presence in their children's lives. They stress the importance of children having both parents, not just a mother and a *visitor*. Their members advocate joint custody, equal time, and equal financial support for and from both parents. In fact, most people on this side of the divorce drama see equality for women as the best thing for fathers. Equality should lead to joint custody and joint financial responsibility.

Fathers' rights groups are located all across the United States and in many countries around the world. Sometimes listed in the phone book under "fathers" or "men's organizations," they can be somewhat hard to find and reach. Your best way to get in touch is over the Internet where fathers' rights groups and men's groups have a strong presence.

If you live in Oregon, Dads Against Discrimination (DADS) is an excellent paralegal advice and support group located in Portland. DADS assists men with the legal paperwork involving custody, child support, and visitation. They also provide encouragement for second wives in their supportive role.

The National Center for Men, originally founded in Old Bethpage, New York, consists of members who believe that it takes two parents to raise children. They provide a crisis line for men, hold rallies, and promote fathers' rights. With chapters located from coast to coast, the National Center for Men holds monthly membership meetings, publishes newsletters, and advocates the reform of biased custody laws.

The Alliance for Non-Custodial Parents' Rights (ANCPR), located in California, promotes the continuation of both parents' involvement in the lives of the children. This groups strongly believes that both the mother and father should continue raising their children on an equal basis after divorce. This is a good group to join over the Internet, even if you live far from California. They have an active email list and web site.

The National Congress for Fathers and Children (NCFC) has promoted joint custody for children since its inception in 1981. It has extensive information available substantiating the importance of keeping fathers involved in the lives of their children. They can provide case citations and sample arguments for those fighting for joint custody.

The Coalition for the Preservation of Fatherhood (CPF) is another volunteer group of both men and women who recognize the need to support fathers. This group, located in Boston, works hard to change present policies that allow ex-wives to turn ex-husbands into throwaway fathers. Their goal is to guarantee that the care of the children is shared by both parents, regardless of their marital status. CPF is affiliated with Parents and Children Together (PACT), Dads Against Discrimination (DADS), and the American Fathers Coalition (AFC).

The American Fathers Coalition is the Federal lobbying arm of The American Coalition for Fathers and Children (ACFC), and is affiliated with many other fathers' groups all across the United States. Their primary purpose is to promote father-inclusive policies on the Federal legislative and regulatory level. The AFC even provides free home pages for children of its members and sponsors a special site just for kids on the Internet.

The Children's Rights Council in Washington, D.C., has created a "Bill of Rights for Children" that describes certain inalienable rights that they think should apply to all children, regardless of their circumstances. This group also stresses the involvement and responsibility of both parents in their children's lives.

These are just a few brief descriptions of the many men's rights, fathers' rights, and children's rights groups found all across the country. Groups such as these also exist in Europe, Canada, and in every country where the rights of fathers are trampled. This is why the Internet is a good source for information; it reaches around the globe.

If you want to get involved, first of all, look in your phone book. Check the Appendix of this book. You will find openings, if you want to find them, doors that will lead you inside, into groups of people who are working for change. If you don't have it, get access to the Internet. You will find second wives' groups, links to associated sites, and ways to contact other second wives and fathers who share your concern.

Many of these groups focus on the issue of child support. It is a problem that affects the life of almost every second wife. Day in and day out, we're inundated with propaganda about deadbeat dads. For all we know from the media, not a single father pays support for his children. Of course, the truth is another story. Most divorced fathers do pay their support in full and on time. The divorced fathers who are allowed an active part in their children's lives usually pay even more, above and beyond requirements.

In a 1995 U.S. Census Bureau *Current Population Survey* (U.S. Department of Commerce, Economics and Statistics Administration/April Supplement, GPO), research showed that 76 percent of custodial mothers who had been awarded child support received payment. Only 63 percent of fathers who were awarded custody as well as child support actually received any payment.

Funny, isn't it? You wouldn't know from the news that a higher percentage of the deadbeats out there are women, would you?

The amount of your husband's child support obligation was decided in a court which favors the divorcing mother, as do all courts today. This one-sided system rendered a judgment which took into consideration the ex-wife's demands and your husband's capacity for financial support. The court might have computed not only what he earns today, but what he might earn tomorrow, and what he *could* earn if he worked overtime and on the weekends. Future raises are often anticipated and included. Pensions are carved up in advance. His future is mortgaged, and so is yours.

It's not that your husband objects to paying support for his children. He wants to take care of them and pay his share. You want him to do so. They are his children. What he and you object to is the uneven nature of the responsibility, putting the whole burden on one side. Here he is, paying an ex-wife who sits on her ass, doing nothing, refusing to get a job, and squandering the child support on everything but the kids. You object to the fact that there is absolutely no accountability demanded for all of this money. You object to the fact that she doesn't share the responsibility for the financial support. You're not the only one!

Gail

"One of the debts, assigned to my husband's ex, is now being garnished from his paycheck, which leaves him approximately $400.00 each month to live on after that and paying his child support. Meanwhile, his ex sits on her butt, threatening to file bankruptcy, and is keeping all the marital property."

Fran

"We have joint custody with my husband's ex-wife as the domicile parent. Since she started working, she's been complaining about the fact that my husband's child support obligation has been reduced. My husband's income varies due to his profession, and now she is accusing him of not working to his capacity."

Most divorced fathers want a little more control. Rather than being reduced to a source of tax-free cash for their ex-wives, they would like some say in how the money is spent and some assurance that it is benefiting the children. While the court orders specify an amount of child support to be paid each month, there are no stipulations requiring ex-wives to spend the money strictly for the children's benefit. Many fathers' rights groups feel there should be some accountability on the ex-wife's part.

A group called the Fathers' Rights and Equality Exchange (F.R.E.E.), of Palo Alto, California, is a not-for-profit organization whose members believe that both mothers and fathers should share equally in the parenting of their children. F.R.E.E. is an advocate for fathers who are eager to take part in raising and supporting their children after divorce. They also took part in the lobbying effort to ban the use of a new mate's income in the determining of child support in California. According to F.R.E.E.'s statistics, fathers are awarded custody in only about ten percent of all divorces.

As mentioned before, often allegations of abuse are used by ex-wives to restrain a father from his children and to undercut a father's bid for custody. At present, a woman can accuse her husband or ex-husband of domestic abuse, and the court takes her strictly at her word. The father can object until he's blue in the face; it makes no damn difference to anyone. The accusation alone is used to deny the father due process and any consideration regarding his children. Quickly, the father is reduced to a simple source of income and questions of custody, visitation, or any other active role in the children's lives are thrown into the garbage, along with the father/child relationship.

One father, driven to fight the system which has denied him any contact whatsoever with his son since April 1996, decided to use the symbol of the Purple Heart, an award for injuries received in the heat of battle, to symbolize his own injury. He painted one purple heart on his house each day that he had not seen his son.

As of December 1997, there were 600 Purple Hearts painted on this father's home. He has publicized his circumstances, as well as those of other fathers who find themselves without contact with their children. His motto is: "Kids Need Fathers, Not Visitors."

Later, this father began to produce Purple Heart Buttons and has sent of 5,500 of these buttons all across the country to other fathers, to be worn as symbols of their missing relationships with their children. After losing his fight with the prejudiced legal system, this father painted his house black, to represent his sorrow.

Some second wives have decided to join together and use their anger constructively, hoping for an eventual positive outcome. They have joined the fathers' rights and men's movements. They have formed their own groups. Everywhere you look you will find second wives who are tired of getting screwed; tired of seeing their husbands getting screwed; and tired of the whole unjust system. Second wives are women, too, and we're too smart to be fooled by "women's advocates" who use the law to screw one another. No one is fooled by their hypocrisy.

In a newspaper article, "Dead Beat Dads' Have New Allies: Second Wives," (October 13, 1996), the assumption is made that all divorced fathers are deadbeats. Describing the work of the Coalition of Parent Support (COPS) in *The Seattle Times*, the article states, "Women . . . represent a new wave in the child-support wars. They are second wives, along with other women, who have become allies in the fathers' rights movement—the late-1980s revolt against a court system that supporters say penalizes men in child-support decisions. In 1994, COPS clinched a stunning legislative victory in California: a bill that exempts a second wife's earnings from any child-support formula."

No one is out there fighting for people who desert their children. The women involved in these organizations are second wives who have experienced firsthand the prejudice against noncustodial fathers. These women want to know when society is going to stop punishing fathers who pay for the sins of fathers who do not. Second wives see the pain that their husbands endure daily. We see the injustice. We hear the political, emotional judges making biased rulings that ignore the facts. We see the way ex-wives manipulate the system at the expense of our husbands, our children, and their own children.

There are millions of second wives in this society and many are joining together to fight the unfairness by forming groups. Some team up with the fathers' rights and the men's movement groups who welcome the help of these women. Some second wives work on their own or set up web sites; others form groups in their own communities to help one another and to affect the system.

The feminist movement originally set out to create opportunities for women and promote equality. However, feminism, like many modern advocacy movements, gained momentum and began to use public sympathy towards women to abuse and dominate men, their perceived enemy, especially in the arena of family law. They have simply gone too far.

On the backs of poor and underprivileged women, feminists, with the help of greedy divorce lawyers, created a powerful set of twisted laws and propaganda that hurts fathers, children, and families. Many men, who may have been good fathers and fine people, found themselves paying for the sins of other men, at the mercy of angry feminist judges who made examples of them.

The feminists are organized, powerful, and willing to lie whenever they feel it advances their cause. They manipulate the media with skewed research; they have nurtured contacts and perfected the use of propaganda. While men hesitate to position themselves as victims in today's "entitlement festival," second wives have no such reluctance. Using the very same techniques that feminists have perfected, second wives are finding out that it is going to be up to them to change things, using the media, the courts, and public opinion, just as the feminists have for years.

The State of Washington has made a small step forward in the consideration of joint custody. In that state, instead of the standard divorce decree, a parenting plan must be filed shortly after the initial filing for divorce. It is a written, detailed account of where the child will reside every day of the year. The parenting plan is meant to provide for more equitable sharing of the time that divorced parents spend with their children. Supposedly, the children do not live with one parent and only visit the other. They reside with each parent separately. However, the court still designates a primary parent and a nonprimary parent (custodial and noncustodial), the primary parent being the mother, in the majority of the cases, and the father being considered the nonprimary parent.

So, calling a parent primary and nonprimary rather than custodial and noncustodial is really no big deal. Euphemisms don't change things. But the idea that a child could have a home with each parent is a breakthrough. Obviously, having two homes, two bedrooms, two sets of toys and clothes is much better for the child than losing a father.

Along with the changes in the custody laws must come a change in child support obligations. How can it be fair that a father should have to pay a set amount of child support to the mother each month when the child lives with each parent for nearly an equal time each year? The child support obligation tables must be adjusted, based on residential time. The father is allowed a deduction for the time that the child spends in his home. Ultimately, we want each parent to pay his and her own equal share of support.

This plan of equal time for both parents is a fine alternative to the familiar arrangement in which the father can only visit his kids every other weekend, and maybe a couple of weeks in the summer, if he's lucky. A written plan helps to clarify times and dates and obligates the mother to comply with visitation. Spelling out details about summer vacation, holidays, and weekends can lead to stability, something all children need. Both parents can plan ahead.

If the plan seems rigid, however, changes have to be made officially and agreed to by both parents. For example, allowances for needs of the children as they grow can be requested and modifications can be made. Changes in work schedules can be accommodated in an organized way. Disruptions to the plan can also be documented and brought to the court's attention.

Those who oppose the parenting plan complain of the possibility of an unscrupulous, noncustodial parent fighting for this type of arrangement, and then failing to live up to his parenting time, thereby forcing the ex-wife to assume more child care costs. Yeah, yeah. They always drag the rats out when someone proposes a little fair dealing. Most fathers would be deliriously happy to have a chance to spend more time with their children and to be able to participate more freely in their children's lives.

This plan of joint residence and equal time with the child is a big step in the right direction. It advances the rights of fathers to be active participants in their children's lives. Also, it distributes the financial responsibility more evenly.

As the fathers' rights groups continue their struggle for justice and equality, more and more second wives are joining them. Eventually, if enough people get involved, things will change for fathers and second families and they can only get better. It's certainly hard to image the system getting much worse than it is now.

10
~All Together Now~

Stepfamilies are far more common than they were twenty or thirty years ago. Times have changed, for better or for worse. Reasons for this are many, but no-fault divorce laws probably had something to do with it all. They were enacted to keep couples who wanted a divorce from lying in court about each other and gathering or making up dirt to prove fault. Whether these laws are good or bad, or whether it was better in the old days when couples were forced to stay married forever, isn't the issue.

Divorce is legal, at least for now. Most people would still like to be able to end an unhappy relationship and have a second chance for a good one. Often we hear people moaning about the "good old days," as if a society can turn back the clock to some magical moment in the perfect past. What about all the illegitimate children who never knew who their real fathers were? What about the back-alley abortions and the illegitimate babies sold to the highest bidder? What about the mistresses and secret boyfriends? What about the children who missed out on their rightful inheritances? What about the miserable people who were trapped and just gave up on life?

We can't go back in time, nor should we. People get married and divorced and married again because they seek the thing that everyone wants: love. We want loving husbands, happy families, and if we have to move the pieces of the puzzle around to achieve those things—it's worth it! Biofamilies are still the fantasy. Original Mom and Dad and kids together. It's great if this works out and sometimes, perhaps half the time, it does. Often as not, however, it takes a bit of juggling the players around to get just the right combination.

For example, a blended family of today might consist of a previously married father with one daughter from his first marriage married to a previously married woman with two sons from her first marriage, who have had another child together since the second marriage. Think of the all relationships here! We have a stepfather, a stepmother, a biological father, a biological mother, stepbrothers, a stepsister, half-brothers, and a half-sister, and the new baby all in one family!

Let's face it. Life is a little more complicated nowadays than it used to be. Unless the divorce rate drops dramatically—and it doesn't look like that is going to happen anytime soon—the stepfamily is a permanent feature on the social horizon.

Forget *The Brady Bunch*. Today's blended families are made up of real people dealing with problems and issues that people in biofamilies never even stop to think about. You might be coping with an ex-wife-from-hell or a deadbeat mom, a variety of weekend visitors, and all kinds of legal and financial difficulties.

You want it to work out the second time around. Life is all about choices, decisions, and consequences. All of our actions have consequences, good or bad. Even if we sit on our asses and do nothing, there are consequences. Once we make a choice, we have to figure out how to live with the consequences of that choice.

As a second wife, you've already made the choice to marry a divorced man. Gradually, you begin to get used to how the dynamics differ in a stepfamily, compared to a biofamily. Perhaps, subconsciously, you would like to recreate your own childhood, in a way, for your children. And yet, you can't expect a blended family to feel, function, and behave in the same way as your childhood biofamily. It will never happen. Blended families are different; not better or worse, just different.

Many second wives and stepmothers were not ready to face the problems and complications of a blended family. Feeling alone and without support, some find their new marriages on the rocks.

Martha

"I cannot begin to describe the emotional hell the last few years in this family have been. If the truth be known, if I had to do it over again, I wouldn't."

Erma

"I'm a second wife and have a few regrets, but not at having married my husband. I regret being a member of a society that allows people to force others to live below poverty levels. I never would have believed such things could happen. It was only after both my brother and my present husband ended up with the shitty end of the stick that reality hit me square in the face."

Terri

"I love my husband with all my heart. However, if I were to be really honest, with myself as well as with others, I would have to say that I would never do it again. I never realized how much more thought would have to go into simple, everyday activities."

Debbie

"The kids are always a problem. The ex is always a problem. We really hoped that when she got married, things would settle down, but she still dwells on the past. We know that things will improve as the kids get older, but the youngest is only ten, so that means stress and pressure for at least another eight years."

Barb

"Would I marry him again? Hell, no. If I had known what we subsequently discovered and what it has cost us, I would have turned and run in the other direction. My own kids have suffered as a consequence of spending over $100,000 in legal fees to fight the ex."

Caroline

"It breaks my heart to say that *no way in hell* would I marry him again. I wouldn't wish that on my worst enemy. I hate to be a party-pooper, but it never ends. The ex will always be there, in the background. Just when you think the problems are about over, here come graduations, weddings, and then grandchildren. It never ends!!!"

Anna

"When my two-year old gives me a hug and a kiss, it is such a reward. His lack of inhibition in showing affection makes it easy for me to love and cherish him. It's so much different with my stepchildren. Their love and loyalty to their mother prevents them from openly showing me any love or affection at all. Even though I understand this, sometimes it's harder to do things for them."

Elaine

"My husband's ex-wife programs my stepson. I can tell as soon as he walks in the door on Friday night. His attitude is disrespectful towards his father and me. I spent the first few years stressing, trying to make everybody happy and comfortable. I eventually learned that I can't take care of anyone if I don't take care of myself."

Sara

"I entered into my marriage being optimistic. I hoped the kids would eventually come around. I always did everything I could to make them feel at home. I treated them like I did my own kids. I spent so much time with these kids. I took them shopping. I took them to the movies. I helped them pick out their mother's birthday presents, and I even took them to visit their grandmother in a nursing home. Not once did I ever receive so much as a birthday card from these kids. Although I know that material gifts are not a way to measure love, it became obvious that I was second in their eyes, compared to their mother, and she's not done anywhere near as much as I have done for them."

Who can really anticipate the everyday difficulties of life in a blended family? How could they have known? It's one thing to be a single woman wanting to be married, and it's quite another to wake up one day and find yourself coping with angry stepchildren and an ex-wife-from-hell.

In spite of that hideous old show *The Brady Bunch*, blended families are not accepted in our society. Oh yes, the TV sitcoms have managed a few polite scenarios, but the truth has not been told. People still want to think of all families as biofamilies. They still crave the comfort of simple relationships and marriages that last a lifetime. After all, what does it say about your family, that it is all blended together? What are the assumptions that people make and the remarks that are exchanged behind your back?

"Is that her real daughter?"

"Do you think that teenage boy really belongs in her home?"

"I wonder if her husband was divorced when she met him."

Some of us react by trying to live in our own little shells, cut off from the outside world. You might think that your problems are unique, that no one knows what you're going through. If you believe that you are on your own in your family and all you can do is make the best of it, let's talk, okay? Now, it's one thing to say you wouldn't chose it all again if you knew then what you know now. But it's quite another to give up.

There is no choice, if we love our husbands and families as we surely must. As second wives, we have to find a way to survive in a society that is quick to blame but slow to help. Some of us are loners; but others among us could use some old-fashioned help now and then.

Problem-solving techniques can be helpful, along with a good strong dose of honesty and willingness to compromise. Let's take a look at some of the common assumptions and reactions that can take place when the going gets rough. For example, how do you think your husband feels?

Here are a few of the things that might be going through his mind.

"She knew I had kids when she married me, so why is she acting like a bitch all of a sudden?"

"She sounds like a snot when she talks to my kids."

"She acts more like a kid than they do sometimes."

"She's obsessed by everything my ex-wife does."

"She doesn't understand how hard it is for me to discipline the kids when I hardly ever get to see them. I'm afraid of losing them again. Why can't she let anything slide?"

"All she does is bitch about money."

Of course, second wives have feelings too.

"Everyone else comes before me."

"I want to have my own baby, but he doesn't want any more kids."

"We can't afford to have a child of our own."

"You'd think he and his ex were still married. All she has to do is call and he jumps."

"All of his money goes to his ex-wife and kids."

"He never disciplines his kids. They're brats."

"He thinks that if he buys his kids something, that means he's a good father."

"He doesn't realize that he'd be on the street if it weren't for my income."

Some of the feelings of parents in blended families seem to fly back and forth, off the wall, and all over the place.

"I should be able to love my stepchildren and treat them as I do my own."

"I shouldn't have to choose between my husband (or wife) and my children."

"Our children could never come between us."

"My mate will always respect my decisions regarding his/her children."

"How could I have gotten myself into this mess?"

"He/She will probably leave me under the strain of it all."

"How can I hold this marriage together for another day? No one understands."

Believe it or not, these are very common feelings. Sometimes love isn't enough to hold the marriage together. It can be too much for either the husband or the wife and when that happens, another family goes down. Both people have to have an extra measure of dedication to success and to each other to make it work. It is a million times more difficult than a conventional marriage.

But it can be done. No one is saying that second marriages can't succeed, and do so magnificently.

Angie

"The counselor asked me what I thought and how I felt about my husband's situation when we decided to marry. I told her that I was aware of it, but that I loved him so much that it didn't matter. I thought I would be able to handle it. She told me that if I had seen her before the marriage, she would have had me rate each pro and con with how strong my emotion was, using a rating of one to five. One is for little emotional feeling, five is for a strong emotional feeling. I've since made my list and surprisingly, I came up with more cons than pros, and the score for the cons was higher as well. Making a list forces you to look at everything a little more rationally. It also helps you realize what your emotions are about each item."

You might want to do this yourself and avoid the hefty fees to the marriage counselor. Get a piece of paper and draw a line down the middle. One column is for pros and one column is for cons. For example, under the pros column, list everything good about your husband and your marriage. You might say, he's very sensitive, kind, caring, loving, considerate, affectionate, a good cook, cleans the bathroom, picks up after himself, is a wonderful father, etc.

Then, under the cons column, list everything you hate about your marriage, your relationship, and your life, such as: Our economic situation sucks; I want to have a baby and we can't afford one; we haven't gone out to dinner in years; my hard-earned money is paying for his ex-wife's vacations; his kids are brats and won't listen; etc.

You and your husband can even do this together sometime, with a little discretion of course. Don't soothe your mood by insulting your husband. The old pro/con list can also be an excellent way to help make decisions that affect the whole family. Often it's quite a surprise to see that what one person is worried about isn't even important to the other.

Gina

"My husband and I spent hundreds of hours analyzing our previous relationships and what went wrong. It became a kind of a hobby, actually. Sometimes we even made a game out of it. My advice is to be open and up-front from the very beginning. It might be hard, but leave your anger from the past behind. It's not your present partner who may have screwed you over so don't be angry with him."

Some of the methods and ideas that make a blended family work are the same as those that make any family function well. The core of the family is the relationship between the husband and wife. If you want your marriage to survive, you must care for your relationship with your husband, not only out of self-interest, but out of sincere love for him.

If the relationship between the husband and wife is strained, the family will suffer. Take time out to be a couple. Every once in a while, just as in a biofamily, take a couple of hours, a day, even a weekend, for the two of you. It's okay to call the babysitter sometimes. You won't go broke from one evening out with your husband. In fact, list that expense as a necessity in your budget. Your family depends on it.

Be sure to take the time to show each other the same love and attention that you did at the beginning of your relationship. The extra responsibilities and arrangements in a blended family might make even a few minutes seem impossible, but you can find a way. Find a way to hold onto the love, help it along during the rough times, and keep it alive, in spite of it all.

Exercise your sense of humor. Give it a good work out at least once a day. We all take ourselves too seriously at times. Laughing helps to release tension, and heaven knows, you have more than enough of that. Negative emotions eat away at us from the inside, giving us indigestion, ulcers, gray hair, and wrinkles. Life is short and we have to live in the moment to a certain extent or we won't be able to hold on. The future is out there, uncertain and rocky. Give yourself a break from worrying about it now and then.

11
~Making It Work~

What if you have to go to court tomorrow to fight a demand for an increase in child support or to fight for visitation rights? How are you going to handle the stress?

First of all, it's costing you time and money. You might have to take a day off from work. The lawyers are all over you, billing you for their worthless time. What will you wear? What will the judge assume about you if you wear this or that? What if the ex-wife gets everything she wants, as usual? Will you explode in a rage at your husband in the car on the way home? Will you blame him or blame yourself?

In ten or fifteen years, it will all be behind you. Really, it's a matter of getting through. If you let it hurt your marriage or your children, you are letting *her* win. You are letting the system work you over. You are fighting yourself, not the enemy.

Somehow you have to do what you have to do in your particular situation, and then you have to let it go. If you're worried about how you and your husband will pay the bills when the increase in child support kicks in, not only will you still have all your bills, but you will have all that extra stress. It doesn't pay to worry or let things bother you to the point where you actually become sick. One way or another, you will make do. People survive and get through worse things. You still have your husband, your children, and the other people in your life who love you. You will find a way. Believe in yourself and in your family, and together, you can make it work. Then you can tackle the unfair situation from a position of strength. And if you go to court and lose your shirt, you can always blame your lawyer.

So enjoy what you can and be happy with what you have. Money is great, but it doesn't necessarily buy happiness. There are plenty of miserable rich people out there, remember. Work at improving your home life and your family relationships. If you can't afford to go the movies, rent videos. Play board games. Keep your loved ones close to you. If it seems like you will never be able to go to Hawaii, so what? You and your husband can have a picnic in bed. When the stepkids are visiting, pack a lunch and take them hiking and have fun. Make dinner together as a family. Watch your favorite shows. Play charades!

When kids act up or misbehave, you discipline them together with your husband and create a predicable set of rules and ways. Just as in any biofamily, you and your husband are the heads of the house. Discuss the kids privately, then act together as a unit. Fighting in front of the stepkids is always a no-no, if you can avoid it.

Communicate with each other regarding each other's expectations and feelings about the behavior of all of the children. This is vital to your marriage, to your relationship with each other, and to the overall welfare of your blended family. Once you and your husband agree on the rules, explain them to the children. Post them on the refrigerator for all to see and stick to them. Chores can be handled in much the same way. Sit down, discuss the daily and weekly chores, delegate them, and post them so nobody can say, "I forgot."

Expect and be prepared for interference from your husband's ex-wife in regard to the standard of discipline observed in your home.

Janice

"Spanking is the issue with my husband's ex. She doesn't agree with corporal punishment. It's only okay with her if the children's father administers the spanking. If I spank *her* kids, to her this is abuse and nothing short of battery. This seems a little contradictory; maybe it's only me. She has threatened to call Child Protective Services if I dare to spank her kids again."

It is not against the law to spank your children, either your biological children or your stepchildren, but it can be dangerous. If your husband's ex-wife threatens to call the authorities, you might find yourself in an ugly mess. Be careful in this case, it might not be worth it and you can probably think of other ways to get your point across.

Kids need to know that there are consequences to their behavior, good or bad. They feel better when there are boundaries. Disrespectful behavior should not be tolerated by you or your husband. When your stepkids do act out, don't take it as a personal insult. When your own kids misbehave, you don't take it personally, do you? Enforce the agreed-upon rules swiftly and fairly.

Never let the children, biological or step, play one parent against the other. This is very destructive to your marriage, and to the whole family. Remember, the blended family is only as strong as the relationship between you and your husband. If your marital relationship fails, the blended family will fall apart.

In any family relationship, bio or blended, we make mistakes. None of us is perfect. So don't be too hard on yourself if you lose your temper, jump to conclusions, or yell when you shouldn't. Most important, admit to yourself, your children, and your stepchildren, when you do make mistakes. Apologize if necessary. It won't belittle you in their eyes at all. It will show them that you're only human, just as they are, and it will earn your children's respect. They, in turn, will be more willing to acknowledge their own mistakes. Honest and open communication is the goal.

One day, your children will grow up and they will leave home. As you anticipate this time, here are some important questions to keep in the back of your mind: When they leave, will they have a sense of responsibility towards themselves and towards others? Will they have the capacity to grow and change and provide for themselves and their future families? Will they be able to find and maintain strong and loving relationships with other people? Will they have the abilities and skills needed to raise children of their own? Contemplating these questions keeps you on the right path as you prepare them for their future.

In the meantime, daily concerns seem to fly at your face with astonishing rapidity. For example, what should your stepchildren call you? Your biological kids will call you Mom, but your stepchildren already have a mom. It might feel awkward, especially if you have your own children calling you Mom, to hear a stepchild call you by your first name. What if you have a baby and your stepchild is calling you by your first name? Will that confuse the baby, as it grows, and cause the baby to call you by your first name, instead of Mommy? It probably won't happen, but some second wives do worry about it.

Talk it over with your husband and decide what you and he are most comfortable with, make a decision, and then inform the kids. "Mommy Susan" might be preferable to just "Susan." Or even "Aunt Susan," which, although incorrect and sort of confusing, at least gives you a title. It's a personal choice, and yours to make. Just don't expect your stepchildren to call you Mom. You might even want to reassure them that you are not trying to take their mother's place by letting them call you by your first name. You are their stepmother, however, and you are also their father's wife. Therefore, you are entitled to and deserving of their respect.

A sense of respect is key, and it pervades the atmosphere during good times and bad. For instance, most members of blended families know that the holidays present a special challenge. Christmas, for example, can be tricky if the kids are with their mother one year and their father the next. Perhaps it's been decided that some stepchildren will be with you and some will be with their mother. Or maybe they're with Mom on Christmas Eve and Dad on Christmas Day.

Mix and match. Mix it up! Every minute doesn't have to be scheduled, but you certainly have the right to know, well in advance, what to expect. Kids, too, should be informed in advance about your expectations. How should they dress? Behave? What should they bring? Waiting until the last minute only adds more stress to an already stressful situation. Of course, you have little control over the ex-wife, and she will do what she will do, but you can be as prepared as possible for the holidays. Then, go with the flow!

Everyone is adjusting to changes in a blended family, including grandparents, cousins, aunts, and uncles. People might feel uncomfortable or miss the "old ways." To overcome this, some stepfamilies make an effort to forge new holiday traditions which are unique to the blended family. Involving the kids in preparations such as baking, making centerpieces, and decorating the house helps to build new memories as well as foster closeness in a blended family. It doesn't matter what you do, as long as the whole family participates. For example, in one blended family, the night before Thanksgiving, everyone helps make side dishes and homemade stuffing for the turkey. Each family member has a job to do, from peeling potatoes to making cornbread to chopping onions. It doesn't matter so much what each child or adult does. The important thing is that you do it together and over time you'll see it become your own family tradition.

With the divorce rate and remarriage rate as high as they are, one would think that by now our society would be more open to the idea of blended families. Unfortunately, this is not true. People can be narrow-minded, bigoted, judgmental, fearful, and critical of any family that doesn't "fit the norm." You've probably sensed this from time to time. Comments come home with the kids about your "unusual" family. Or you overhear a remark such as, *"How many people actually live in that house?"* You know that some people in biofamilies think that your family is not a "legitimate" family or that something about it is wrong or immoral. This is part of the hassle that second wives endure and all you can do is keep your head up and recognize that it doesn't matter what other people think as long as you are strong and you know that your family is exactly what a family should be.

Remember all those family pictures your parents had taken when you were a child? Remember getting all dressed up only to spend half a day sitting around in some boring photography studio? Sure, you might laugh at those pictures today, but your parents probably treasure them.

Aren't you glad they have those pictures? They're memories of your family from a time that no longer exists. People always say that children grow up too fast and, perhaps it is true. It might be hard to imagine your stepchildren growing up too fast, but one day old pictures of their little faces are going to bring back some memories for you too.

Blended families should have their family picture taken once a year, just as any biofamily would. It makes a big difference, especially to kids who visit only every other weekend, to see their faces in the family picture on the wall. It helps lessen that uncomfortable I'm-just-a-visitor feeling and gives them, instead, a sense of belonging.

Sometimes it's easier to blend the new family together if the whole family moves into a different home. In spite of the inconvenience and expense, this is one of those efforts that often proves to be worthwhile in the long run. The new place is everybody's home, and a fresh start for everyone. Territories are redefined. Arrangements are made with everyone in mind. Psychologically, it can be very, very good for the whole family.

Our society is slow to change and slow to accept change. However, stepfamily support groups are beginning to spring up, many of them founded by second wives weary of the stereotypes and tired of the bullshit. One second wife has founded a support group especially for Christians involved with the issues of divorce and remarriage. Her success, along with her husband, in making their new marriage and family work motivated her to help others navigate this bumpy road. The group now publishes a monthly newsletter, "Life's Landmines to Landscapes," especially for blended families. It's always helpful and inspiring to read about others who have endured some of the same trials and challenges as you have and weathered them well.

Sandy

"Make the family number one. Spend time with one another, try to ease the stress. Remember, if it's hard on you, it's hard your husband and children, too. It's like a big lifeboat . . . don't let it sink."

12

~The Golden Years~

*A*ge enters into the life of a second wife in a variety of ways. In one respect, you might be a second wife in her sixties or seventies yourself. Or you might get married to a man who is old enough to be a grandpa. Age is also a consideration even if you and your husband are the same age and relatively young because your blended family now possibly includes grandparents, in-laws, and other members of your parents' generation.

As an older second wife, you have unique concerns and considerations. We often assume that our retirement and later years will be calm and peaceful. Just picture it: the children have grown up and moved away; the relationships have settled into place; and the day-to-day struggle to survive has eased itself into a predictable routine. Ahhh, what a relief, finally. Unless, of course, you decide to get married again.

First of all, grown children can be just as difficult, if not worse than younger ones, when it comes to their reactions to their parents' remarriage. Subtlety probably won't be their first priority, especially if their mother, your husband's ex-wife, sits on a majestic throne in their mind's eye. The glorious ex-wife becomes downright angelic, if Dad decides to remarry after a long, long marriage to *her*.

Suppose you are significantly younger than your new husband. His children automatically assume that you're a gold digger, even if you're thirty-five. But if you're older than your new husband, then Dad's gone out of his mind! Who will pay your imminent medical bills? Whether or not an age difference is involved, your new grown-up stepchildren will probably feel threatened by the marriage and by you.

Your biological children might object, as well. They've probably met with the accountant about providing for your care. Now what? They've got their eye on the house; what's going to happen with it? His children, your children. They're all grown and expecting things to follow the plans that they have devised for *their* parents. Your remarriage will cause them anxiety about money, about motives, and about anything else you can imagine.

You will probably have to endure some bold interrogations about your intentions.

"Mom, are you sure you want to get married again? After all, you are 60 years old, you know. Does he have kids? How do they feel about the marriage? Did he divorce his wife or did she die? What are we supposed to call him? How old is he? You need to be careful, you know. There are unscrupulous men out there waiting to take advantage of lonely older women. He could be after your money. Do you plan to sell the house? What about all of Dad's stuff? Does he have grandchildren? Does he drink?"

Don't be too offended. Your new husband will be experiencing the same kind of ruthless cross-examination from his grown children.

"Dad, did it ever cross your mind that she might be after your money? Does she have kids? Are you going to change your will? What about the house? What about Mom's stuff? What is the point of getting married again anyway, especially at your age?"

As an older second wife, you need not be so concerned with the everyday struggles with visitation, child support, and the molding of little minds. However, you will have to contend with the suspicion and judgment of grown children which can be painful and troubling.

So, you've just gotten married. Maybe you finally found the man of your dreams after all these years. Years of sacrifice for your children who now have the nerve to question you. Come on! A gold digger? Aren't gold diggers supposed to be brainless young bimbos? It's insulting! His children are at you, too. Both sets at once! Even worse is their brazen anticipation of your husband's death. To you, he's your husband, a vibrant and sexy man. You're just beginning a life together. They act as if he's on death's doorstep, and your very presence threatens their precious inheritance. It's undeniably disgusting.

Not all grown children will act this way. Some of them will be genuinely happy for you. However, it's the grown children, either yours or his, who disrespect you that cause you the most grief. How does your husband feel about it? Probably, he understands why his children are concerned and their loyalty to their mother, but he should also demand that they control themselves around you. You are his wife and you deserve some respect. As in any second marriage, you and your husband must talk privately and away from the children and then present a united front. It is the only way.

At times, you might find yourself feeling a bit insecure when you think about your husband's former wife, especially if they had a long marriage and good life-style. If she cleaned him out during the divorce, you might feel as if you are somehow depriving him of the better life he once enjoyed. Push that thought out right of your mind! If your husband cared more about money and luxury than about you, he would still be married to that bitch. He chose you.

Darla

"I feel foolishly insecure, sometimes. I am envious of my husband's past life with her. They lived quite an extravagant life-style, traveled, and did so many things that he and I will never be able to do. I feel second-rate, somehow. It's hard to put my feelings into words. Even though they were all in their twenties, his kids made their disapproval of our marriage explicitly clear.

"Bobby was so patient with me, until one day when he finally said, 'Damn it. I divorced the bitch because that's exactly what she was. I never knew from one day to the next what mood she would be in when I got home from work. Nothing made her happy, not a goddamn thing. I don't care about the damn house. It takes too long to clean anyway.' He kind of shocked me but I guess that's what I really needed. I finally got over my insecurities and we are content and happy."

In some ways, older second wives face challenges that no one wants to even talk about. Age-related issues are thorny enough without throwing in all the problems that second wives share. And you thought that once your kids grew up, your worries would be over!

As a "senior citizen" you have to recognize that your children probably feel obligated to look after your welfare. They might treat you like a child. They might be so condescending that they make you want to throw up. But they are your babies and you love them. You're not going to stop tolerating them at this point.

So, even though they're clearly overstepping their boundaries, so to speak, try to put your cynicism aside—at least they care! Sit down and have a long talk with them.

Thank them for their interest, but put your foot down. Make it clear that you will not tolerate any interference or insults.

Grace

"We just ignore the petty comments. It's really not worth getting upset over. Bill and I have each other, we're happy, and the kids will just have to deal with that. We have the grandkids over as often as we can and we're always available for babysitting so the parents can have a night out. But we've earned our place in life and our freedom."

Usually grown children will adapt and then accept your situation. They might even get used to it and start to hang around. Everyone knows that grandparents make the best babysitters.

Julie

"There have been times when I've had to say no to requests for overnight babysitting, because we do have a life of our own. Sometimes we have plans and actually go out. It's only a matter of mutual respect that advance notice be given if our kids want us to keep the grandkids. Still, I can't deny that I love having the kids here, especially without their parents around."

Maybe your husband is the senior citizen in the marriage and you are much younger than he is, in fact, you're the same age as most other second wives. You might be about the same age as his grown children! Talk about awkward. When you meet his daughter she stands face to face with you and sarcastically asks if she's supposed to call you "Mom."

Yours is a relationship that really makes people angry and it's a good idea to brace yourself for the nasty reactions that will undoubtedly be coming your way.

Mary

"Our relationship was great regardless of our age difference, until Joe's kids came to visit one Christmas. Then it was like we were all kids to him. He turned into the father-figure from hell. He nagged and questioned his kids about their jobs, bossed them around, and even started ordering me around. That lasted all of one afternoon. After everyone went to bed the first night, I told him I was his wife, not his child. Then I told him that his children were adults now, not little kids. He had no right to question their decisions about anything. I told him that I understood his concern but, unless they asked for his opinion, it was none of his damn business. The visit went much better after that."

Other people, outside of your marriage, will probably make remarks about your husband's mid-life crisis or about your father-figure problem, but you can just go right past all of that bullshit. In some ways, you have the ideal second-wife life because you and your husband have all kinds of freedom. You don't have to worry about raising his kids; they're already grown. If they don't like you or the fact that you are married to their father, whose problem is that? They have to get over it, not you. You don't have to endure mind-blowingly high child support payments or the whole visitation ordeal. You have your time with your husband, limited though it may ultimately be, and you can enjoy it. You could even have a baby together, if you both want to, and you'll probably be able to afford it. Wow!

Second wives come in all sizes, ages, shapes, and styles. Maybe you've been a second wife for a good long time by now. You're in your sixties and should probably have a black belt by now in this blended family business. Believe it or not, it's not really over until it's over. One day you wake up to find the ex-wife-from-hell rearing her ugly head again!

Does she ever go away? Has she changed one bit? Of course not! On the contrary, she's used all these years to perfect her techniques. Yes, she's gotten every penny out of your and your husband that she could possibly get. Yes, she's already done everything an ex-wife-from-hell could do to disrupt your lives. But you've managed to raise your children and her children and, by God, you're ready to relax with your husband now.

Yet, old habits do die hard. The children may be grown, but Hecuba has herself another set of young minds to manipulate now—the grandchildren. It's *déja vu*. See her fill their young minds with lies, insults, and suspicions. See her try to destroy one of life's very best treasures, the love of grandchildren.

Suddenly little Amanda begins to ask and say all kinds of unexpected things.

"Grandpa, why did you divorce Grandma? She says divorce is a sin."

"You're not our real grandma, you know."

"My real grandma says that Grandpa is in his second childhood. What does that mean?"

You'll probably want to suppress any initial reaction that might be tinged with anger, such as, *"It's none of your damn business. Besides, your real grandma is a vile bitch and she can have you, you demon spawns from hell."* Bite your tongue, as hard as it may be, and remember that living well is the best revenge. Smile at the little imps. Tell them that since the divorce happened so long ago, the reason for it isn't important anymore.

It's like a rerun of an old, bad movie. Somehow, though, it's kind of nice to know that she's still out there, fuming about you after all these years. Here you are in the house with your husband, still happily married. And there she is, still trying to cause you trouble and pain. There's something comforting about it, in a twisted kind of way. She can't hurt you anymore, really, but she's still trying. Pretty pathetic. You smile to yourself.

The other side of the age issue for today's second wife revolves around the older people in your life and their relationships to their grandchildren. Now you've got your parents, your husband's parents, and perhaps even his ex-wife's parents to reckon with. Grandparents often become an issue in divorce.

Since 75 percent of all divorces are filed by wives and husbands are the ones left behind, chances are your husband's parents might well be a couple of broken-hearted grandparents. For his biweekly visits or measly two weeks in the summer, how much time do you think Gramps and Nanny get to spend with their little treasure? Nada.

Here is yet another avenue for torture. The ex-wife-from-hell knows very well how much his parents love their grandchild. She knows they'll do anything or pay anything to be close. She can rake them over the coals almost as ruthlessly as she does your husband by poisoning the children's minds, by wrecking up planned visits, by telling evil lies about the grandparents. She can do whatever she damn well pleases because grandparents have no say and no control over her.

These days, some grandparents are getting pretty fed up with their sons' ex-wives. They don't like losing contact with their grandchildren any more than they like seeing their son jerked around by a woman they wish he'd never married in the first place.

Some grandparents have taken their cases to court to preserve their rights to be with their grandchildren. Perhaps because judges and lawyers don't seem to hate grandparents as much as they hate fathers, the courts have begun to consider the visitation rights of grandparents.

Let's face it, how evil and selfish can an ex-wife get? To deprive a child of a loving grandparent should be a crime. Grandparents are very important to children.

Cindy

"My grandfather spent a lot of time with me. My mother worked two jobs and she was always tired. My grandfather taught me how to play poker when I was sick with rheumatic fever, chicken pox, and measles. I think back on how I probably pestered the hell out of him, but not once did he ever get impatient or angry with me. He showed me how to plant a garden, took me to the store, taught me how to shop, and listened to me. He was the guiding force in my life. I hate to think where I would be today if I hadn't had such a person in my life."

Of course, if fathers were given equal time with their children then the grandparents wouldn't have a problem. They could simply come over or join in during the times when the kids are with their dad. But in today's world, where fathers are reduced to mere visitors in their children's lives, where visitation itself is often denied and fraught with pain and anger, and where ex-wives rule the courtrooms, grandparents usually come last on the list of things to work out.

This does not mean that your husband's ex-wife won't try to hit them up for money or use them as free babysitters when it's convenient for her. She might play their love for her child for all its worth. Again, there isn't much you or they can do about it. Until the system changes and divorce becomes more fair and less torturous, they can only state their cases in court and hope for the best.

I encourage grandparents to sue for custody and visitation rights when their sons lose their children to ex-wives-from-hell. After all, the more litigation for the cause of fair treatment, the better. Each time a father or his parents sue an ex-wife for custody, it makes a little chink in the wall. Someday, many, many chinks in the wall might create an opening for some small child to pass through.

~Conclusion~

Second wives. We're not so bad. We're not witches. (First wives are!) We are not evil temptresses out to destroy marriages and tear families apart. We are not bimbos, gold diggers or trophies. We are not evil stepmothers.

Second wives are normal women, including all of the women who raised their voices to contribute to this book. Second wives are all around us. Practically every other woman you meet is a second wife. She doesn't advertise it, of course. When you meet a second wife, she doesn't shake your hand and say, "Hi, I'm Sandy and I'm a second wife." That would be weird. But open the door just a crack, one little comment about the ex, or a "weekend with the kids," and you'll see. A flood will follow. Suddenly, you and Sandy have a lot in common.

We need one another. We need to reach out, and hang out, and pretend to barf together over movies that make the first wives look like saints. We need to joke around, and help one another, and talk about it on the bad days, saying, "Yeah, I know what you're going through."

Don't forget, also, to turn to your husband. Look to him for the help you need. Ask him for it; he can't read your mind. And he loves you. You are the one he chose. You two are together because you love and treasure each other. Whatever you endure is endurable because you have each other in your life.

Believe it or not, many women go through life without really knowing what it is like to be loved. They can only dream of the adoration and respect that your husband gives you every day. You are the embodiment of his hopes and dreams for the future. You are the one who knows him, who understands, and who enjoys the full power and depth of his love. You are the correction of a bad mistake.

If that's not enough to make you feel great, ask yourself what it would take. Money? A baby? A life free of the ex-wife-from-hell? Sure, all of the above or any of the above would be a big improvement. There are days when we swear that we just can't take it anymore. We can't go on fighting this fight. We can't work any more hours; we can't try any harder. And yet, we somehow do manage to get through the day. We manage to love our children, all of them, and our husbands. We tie things together. We take care of business and we hang in there.

Sometimes we snicker at those women out there who complain about their bad memories or some dirty joke told at the office. *Cry me a river, honey.* Some people don't know what real trouble is all about. They'd get over their bi-polar allergic dysfunctional problems pretty damn quick if they had lawyers hounding them every day or an ex-wife-from-hell grabbing all their money, wouldn't they? Really puts things in perspective.

What are we here for anyway? To accumulate belongings? To prove something to our parents or friends or neighbors? To be thin and rich and famous? (Okay, I'll take that one.) The truth is that it doesn't amount to much, any of it, without love in our lives. We have husbands who truly love us and whom we love deeply. We have children galore! Yours, mine, and ours. What else is there really?

Again, I must say that if you haven't yet had your own baby and your husband is open to it, don't wait around for the bank account to fill up first. Even though it might be a huge strain on you financially, it will be a worse strain later to have felt that you lost your chance. And there's nothing like the face of your own little baby to make you feel like life is worth living. So, if you can do it and you want it, go for it!

Finally, let's work harder to help one another. The resources in the Appendix offer many, many opportunities to reach out to other second wives, fathers' rights groups, and other organizations. We must lift our voices. We must join together and speak out, demanding changes. If we fail to do it, truly, we have only ourselves to blame for the perpetuation of the status quo.

I hope that this book will help bring us together and get people talking about second wives. I want to thank all of the second wives and others who contributed their sincere thoughts and feelings to this book. Perhaps it will inspire more second wives to go on record and join in the efforts to change the brutality of the divorce and family courts.

It is time for a change. Speak out. Write letters. Form groups. Let's compete head-on with the ones who created this miserable system and let's beat 'em at their own game!

The various groups organized by and for second wives are a great place to begin, as are the many stepfamily associations. The numerous fathers' rights groups are also an excellent resource for second wives who witness the injustice of our court system which is determined to drive fathers out of the lives of their children. Fathers' rights groups are located all across the country, and all of them have contacts with many more organizations. Don't forget about the Internet, either.

Sometimes, I know, it takes so much energy just to survive and fight for the right to exist each day that it's hard to even imagine adding more to our plate. Organizing and meeting and writing and faxing . . . who has time? But what if we don't do it? What will happen then? It will only get worse. When our sons grow up, what chance will they have for a family life? What about our daughters? Do we want them to grow up and go through this?

No. No. No. We have to find time and we have to make the effort. It's not going to change until we change it, and, yes, we will change it. Yes, we will.

One second wife at a time.

———

~*Appendix*~

Alliance for Non-Custodial Parents' Rights (ANCPR)
    9903 Santa Monica Blvd., Suite 267
    Beverly Hills, CA 90212
    http://www.ancpr.org/ancprindex.html

American Fathers Coalition (AFC)
    1718 M Street, NW, Suite 187
    Washington, DC 20036   1-800-978-DADS
    http://www.erols.com/afc/ *or* http:www.acfc.org

Blended Family Resource Guide
    http://www.geocities.com/Heartland/Meadows/1423
    /resources.html

Children's Rights Council
    220 I Street NE, Rm 200
    Washington, DC 20002-4307
    (202) 547-6227 800-747-KIDS
    http://www.vix.com/crc/rights.htm

Coalition of Parent Support (COPS)
    10811 Alderbrook Lane, Cupertino, CA 95014
    (408) 450-3552, (415) 965-7471(fax)
    http://bennett.com/COPS/chapters.htm

The Coalition for the Preservation of Fatherhood (CPF)
    14 Beacon Street, Suite 421, Boston, MA 02108 *or*
    P.O. Box 8051, Boston, MA 02114
    (617) 723-DADS *or* (617) 649-1906 (message phone)
    FATHERS-L@HOME.EASE.LSOFT.COM
    http://www.tiac.net/users/sbasile/CPF

Dads Against Discrimination (DADS)
    320 SW Stark St. Portland, OR 97204
    (503) 222-1111/(800) 323-7872
    http://www.teleport.com/~dads

Divorce Helpline Webworks
    (408) 426-0195 Fax (408) 426-0509
    http://www.divorcehelp.com/
    inbox@divorcehelp.com

DivorceNet, advice on child support, custody, visitation, alimony
    http://www.divorcenet.com

The Divorce Page Index of Resources
    http://hughson.com/resources.html

Family Law Advisor Home Page
    http://www.divorcenet.com/Fla-map.html

Fathering Magazine, an online magazine with some articles about
    divorce and fathers' issues
    http://www.Fathermag.com/features.html

Fathers' Hotline/Texas Fathers for Equal Rights
    807 Brazos, Suite 315, Austin, TX 78701
    (512) 472-DADS/(512) 499-8056 fax
    tfa@menhotline.org

Fathers' Resource Center
    430 Oak Grove Street, Suite B3
    Minneapolis, MN 55403   (612) 874-1509
    frc@winternet.com

Fathers' Rights and Equality Exchange (F.R.E.E.)
    701 Welch Road, #323, Palo Alto, CA 94304
    (415) 853-6877
    shedevil@vix.com, http://www.vix.com/free/index.html

Federal Office of Child Support Enforcement Home Page
    http://www.acf.dhs.gov:80/programs/CSE/fct

The Kids Corner/ Children's Rights Coalition of Austin, TX
    P.O. Box 12961, Austin, TX 78711
    http://www.erols.com/afc/kids/kids.htm

Lee's Men's Issue Page is a divorced father's personal web page with many, many links to groups in Georgia, Tennessee, Florida, Wisconsin, Ohio, California, and Washington
http://www.inetnow.net/~leehunt/men.html

Men's Defense Association
17854 Lyons Street, #101, Forest Lake, MN 55025-8107
MensDefens@aol.com *or* http://www.mensdefense.org

Mogg, Debra S. "Life's Landmines to Landscapes," newsletter and ministry for stepfamilies
100 W. Esplanade Avenue, Suite 102-143
Kenner, LA 70065 (504) 443-1449 Lifestep@aol.com
http://members.aol.com/lifestep/index.htm

Moms Online, a "home for moms in cyberspace." Many links, and a message board for stepfamilies
http://www.momsonline.com

My Guardian Angel, a support group for children of divorce
3701 W. Northwest Hwy, Suite 150, Dallas, TX 75220
(214) 350-3396

The National Center for Fathering
1-800-593-DADS http://www.fathers.com

The National Center for Men
P.O. Box 555, Old Bethpage, NY 11804
(516) 942-2020   ncmen@teleport.com

The National Center for Men, Oregon Chapter
P.O. Box 6481, Portland, OR 97228-6481
(503) 224-9477 ncmen@teleport.com
http://www.teleport.com/index.htm

National Congress for Fathers and Children (NCFC)
9454 Wilshire Blvd., #207, Beverly Hills, CA 90212
(310) 247-6051 *or* 1-800-SEE-DADS
http://www.primenet.com/ncfc

National Father Initiative
1 Bank Street, Suite 160
Gaithersburg, MD 20878 (310) 948-0599
http://www.vix.com/pub/men/orgs/writeups/nfi.html

Non-Custodial Parents' Resource Page
http://www.Bayou.com/~ncfc

Parents for Better Family Solutions (PBFS of New Jersey)
384 Roslyn Avenue, New Milford, NJ 07646
http://ourworld.compuserve.com/homepages/JBelthoff
/pbfs.htm

Second Wives Club, an informal group of second wives who
communicate with one another by email. joli@aol.com

Second Wives Crusade, a great site for second wives and blended
families. http://www.secondwives.org

Step Family Association of America
215 Centennial Mall South, Suite 212
Lincoln, NE 68055 (402) 477-7837

Stepfamily Association of Illinois (SAI)
P.O. Box 3124, Oak Park, IL 60303 (708) 848-0909
http://www.parentsplace.com/readroom/stepfamily
index.html

The Stepfamily Foundation
333 West End Avenue, New York, NY 10023
(212) 877-3244, (212) 362-7030 (fax)
(212) 744-6924 Crisis line/Hotline
(212) 799-STEP 24-hour information line
http://www.stepfamily.org

Stepmom's Retreat, K. C. Blake
http://www.geocities.com/Heartland/Plains/6663
kcblake@aol.com

United Fathers of America
        6360 Van Nuys, #8
        Van Nuys, CA 91401 (818) 981-9321
        http://www.fathersunited.com.
        info@unitedfathers.com

Victims of Child Abuse Laws (VOCAL)
        4584 Appleton Avenue, Jacksonville, FL 32210
        (904) 381-7080
        http://www.vocal.org

Wade, Jeanine, Ph.D. "Hints for Divorcing Parents"
        http://www.realtime.net/~mmjw/jw.htm

Washington Families for Noncustodial Rights
        P.O. Box 68401, Seattle, WA 98168
        (206) 233-9472 (206) 233-9475 fax
        Membership information: 1-800-795-7677

The World Wide Web Virtual Library
        Men's Movement Organizations
        http://www.vix.com/men/orgs.html

Bibliography

Belsky, Gary. "The Brady Bunch of the 1990's." *Money* 2 Dec. 1996: 127-133.

Bisnaire, L., P. Firestone, and D. Rynard. "Factors Associated with Academic Achievement in Children Following Parental Separation." *The American Journal of Orthopsychiatry* 60.1(1990).

Block, Jack. "Parental Functioning and the Home Environment in Families of Divorce." *The Journal of the American Academy of Child and Adolescent Psychiatry*, p.27.

Covington, Lee. *How to Dump Your Wife.* Seattle: Fender Publishing Company, 1996.

Dateline NBC. NBC, New York. 15 Dec. 1997.

Fetzner, William N. "Fathers Deserve Equal Justice." *The Christian Science Monitor* 22 June 1990.

Furstenberg, F. and A. Cherlin. *Divided Families.* Boston: Harvard UP, 1991.

Gibbs, Nancy. "An Antique Law Sends Tremors Through Many a Heart." *Time* 18 Aug. 1997:50+.

Kalter, J. "Long-Term Effects of Divorce on Children: A Developmental Vulnerability Model." *The American Journal of Orthopsychiatry* 57.4 (1987).

Kelly, Joan. *Joint Custody and Shared Parenting.* 2nd ed. New York: Guilford Press, 1991.

Laubinger v. Massachusetts Department of Revenue/Child Support Enforcement, Massachusetts Appeals Court, 95-P-1441.

Rubin, Bonnie Miller. " 'Dead Beat Dads' Have New Allies: Second Wives." *The Seattle Times* 13 Oct. 1996: A16.

U. S. Department of Commerce, Economics and Statistics Administration. *Current Population Survey.* April Supplement. Washington, DC: GPO, 1995.

U. S. Department of Health and Human Services, National Center for Health Statistics. *Survey on Child Health.* Washington, DC 1993.

U. S. Department of Justice. *Survey of Inmate Characteristics* U.S. Bureau of Justice Statistics, Washington, DC: GPO, 1990.

About the Author

Christine Thomas is a self-employed writer and researcher, working at home amidst the crayons and the cracker crumbs. Using the Internet, she interviewed scores of second wives, asking them questions and seeking answers. Nevertheless, many of the ideas and suggestions in this book are the product of her own harrowing and yet enlightening personal experiences both as a second wife and as a stepmother.

Ms. Thomas lives in southern Arizona with her blended family.

Notes

Notes

Notes

Notes

Notes